t
happiness
cure

ALSO BY ANDERS HANSEN

The ADHD Advantage

The Mind-Body Method

The Attention Fix

the happiness cure

Why You're Not Built
for Constant Happiness, and
How to Enjoy the Journey

Dr. Anders Hansen

Zeitgeist • New York

Published in the United States by Zeitgeist™,
an imprint and division of Penguin Random House LLC, New York.
zeitgeistpublishing.com

Zeitgeist™ is a trademark of Penguin Random House LLC.

Originally published in Swedish as DEPPHJÄRNAN in 2021
by Bonnier Fakta, Stockholm, Sweden.
Copyright © 2021 by Anders Hansen.
This translation published in the United Kingdom by Vermilion, an imprint of Ebury Publishing, a division of Penguin Random House Ltd., London in 2023.
Ebury is part of the Penguin Random House group of companies.

Layout and illustrations copyright © by Lisa Zachrisson

Published by arrangement with Salomonsson Agency

ISBN: 9780593885840
Ebook ISBN: 9780593886182

Printed in the United States of America
1st Printing

First US Edition

Dedicated to

Vanja Hansen
Hans-Åke Hansen (1940–2011)
Björn Hansen

Before brains, the universe was free of pain and anxiety.

ROGER W. SPERRY

THIS BOOK LOOKS AT why, even when we have things so good, so many people seem to be struggling with their mental health. It deals with milder forms of depression and anxiety, but not bipolar disorder or schizophrenia. There are two reasons for this. First and foremost, bipolar disorder and schizophrenia are far too complex to explore within the scope of a single popular science book. Secondly, the mental health problems that appear to be on the rise in today's society tend to be milder forms of mental illness. Schizophrenia and severe forms of bipolar disorder are not on the rise, and therefore the arguments highlighted here are not applicable to them. In this book, I present a biological way of viewing our mental and physical health that I know from experience many people find helpful. If you are feeling down, seek professional help. And if you are taking any medication for a psychiatric condition, always consult your doctor first before making any changes.

CONTENTS

WHY DO WE FEEL SO BAD WHEN WE HAVE IT SO GOOD?

YOU WILL PROBABLY feel down from time to time. Perhaps you suffer from mild anxiety, or occasionally find yourself struck by utter, debilitating panic. Perhaps at one point in your life things felt so bleak that you could hardly get yourself out of bed. Come to think of it, this is all a little strange, as between our ears we hold a biological marvel so advanced it should be able to cope with . . . well, *anything*.

Your ever-changing, remarkably dynamic brain consists of 86 billion cells with at least *100 trillion connections*. These create intricate networks that govern all of the body's organs, all while processing, interpreting and prioritizing an endless stream of sensory impressions. Your brain can store the information equivalent of 11,000 libraries packed full of books—that's how much your memory can actually hold. And yet, within a fraction of a second it can pull up the most relevant information—even if decades have passed since it was stored—and relate that to what you are currently experiencing.

So, if your brain can do all this, why can't it manage a simple task like making you feel fantastic all the time? Why must it insist on putting a wrench in your emotional works? This riddle is made all the more cryptic when we consider that we are living in an age of unparalleled abundance that would have knocked the socks off pretty much any king, queen, emperor and pharaoh in history. We are living longer, healthier lives than ever before, and should we ever find ourselves the slightest bit bored, the planet's collective knowledge and entertainment are never more than a few taps away.

Still, even though we have never had it so good, many of us appear to be struggling. Hardly a day goes by without an alarming report on the rise in mental health problems. In the US, one in eight adults is taking antidepressants. The World Health Organization estimates that 284 million people in the world have an anxiety disorder, while 280 million suffer from depression. It is feared that within a matter of years depression will generate a greater global burden of disease than any other illness.

So why do we feel so bad when we have it so good? This is a question that has nagged me throughout my career. Do 284 million people have a sickness in their brain? Are one in eight adults lacking in certain neurotransmitters?

Why do we feel so bad when we have it so good? This is a question that has nagged me throughout my career.

It was only when I realized that we can't simply work from where we are today, but must also take stock of where we have been, that a new way of thinking came to me—an approach that not only gives us a deeper understanding of our emotional lives, but also opens up new ways to improve them. I believe that the answer to why we feel so bad when we have it so good is that we have forgotten that we are biological beings. That's why in this book we will be looking at our emotional life and well-being from a neurobiological perspective, exploring why the brain works the way it does. Having worked with thousands of patients, I have seen first-hand how valuable this knowledge can be. It gives us a deeper insight into what we need to prioritize to feel as good as we can. It also helps us to understand ourselves better, which in turn makes us kinder to ourselves.

First up, we are going to look at what happens in our brains when we experience common mental health problems —depression and anxiety—and why this can sometimes be a sign of health as opposed to sickness. We will then turn our attention to what we can do to manage these problems. After that, we will explore whether we really do feel worse than we did before, and how a biological outlook on our emotional lives could change this. Finally, we will try to pinpoint what it is that makes us happy.

But let's start from the beginning—literally.

CHAPTER 1

WE ARE THE SURVIVORS!

Extinction is the rule. Survival is the exception.

CARL SAGAN

LET'S WIND THE CLOCK BACK some 250,000 years and transport ourselves to East Africa. Here we meet a woman, who we'll call Eve. Eve looks like you and me, and she lives with a hundred or so other people who spend their days gathering food in the form of edible plants and hunting wild animals. Eve has had seven children, but four of them have died: one son died during birth, a daughter from a severe infection, another daughter from a fall and a teenage son from being drawn into a conflict and killed. Three of Eve's children did, however, reach adulthood, and they have a total of eight children. Of these, four will reach adulthood and they, in turn, will have their own children.

Repeat this over 10,000 generations and you will find Eve's great-great-great-great- (etc.) grandchildren. And who are they? Well, you and me. We are the descendants of the few who didn't die in childbirth, whose infections managed to heal and who avoided bleeding out from wounds, succumbing to starvation, getting murdered or being mauled to death by a predator. You and I are the latest links in an unbroken chain of the people who were left standing after the smoke of the battlefield, infectious diseases and disastrous famines had passed.

When we think about it, it's obvious that none of your forefathers or foremothers could have died before bringing a child into this world. But this has consequences that are far less obvious. Those of Eve's descendants who reacted keenly to dangers and were particularly wary about that rustling in the bushes—which could have been a lion—had better odds of survival. And because you and I are descended from these survivors, we too have a heightened alertness to danger. Similarly, those of our ancestors who had a strong immune system had a greater chance of surviving an infectious disease, which is why most of us have excellent immune systems—even if it doesn't always feel that way come February.

One further consequence of all this relates to our psychological traits. You see, those of Eve's descendants who had mental qualities that helped them to survive had a greater chance of doing just that, and as a result you and I still bear those very same qualities.

That we have an unbroken chain of survivors behind us, and that not one of them was killed by a lion, stumbled off the edge of a cliff or starved before they could procreate, should make us superhuman. We should be as smart as two-time Nobel Prize winner Marie Curie, as wise as spiritual leader Mahatma Gandhi and as cool as Jack Bauer in the TV series *24*. But are we really all that?

The fittest

The expression "survival of the fittest" brings to mind someone who is mentally and physically in tip-top condition. But when it comes to human evolution, this "fitness" isn't so much about good mental or physical shape as our *fitness for the environment we live in*. Which is why we can't view the qualities that helped our ancestors to survive and reproduce in light of the world we live in now. Instead, we must view them in the context of the world we have inhabited for almost all of human history.

Type of society	Hunter-gatherer	Agrarian	Industrial	Information
Period	250,000–10,000 BCE	10,000 BCE–1800 CE	1800–1990	1990–
Life expectancy at birth	c. 33 years	c. 33 years	35 years (1800) 77 years (1990)	82 years (Europe, 2020)
Most common causes of death	Infections, starvation, murder, blood loss, childbirth	Infections, starvation, murder, blood loss, childbirth	Infections, childbirth, pollution, cardiovascular disease, cancer	Cardiovascular disease, cancer, stroke
Percentage of our history	96%	3.9%	0.08%	0.02%

Our bodies are designed for survival and reproduction, not health. Our brains are designed for survival and reproduction, not well-being.

There was no intrinsic value to Eve's children being strong, healthy, happy, kind, well-adjusted or smart; by evolution's crude logic only two things mattered: survival and reproduction. This single realization has come to completely transform the way I view humankind. Our bodies are designed for survival and reproduction, not health. Our brains are designed for survival and reproduction, not well-being. The way you feel, the sort of person you are and whether you have friends, food, a roof over your head or any other resources—none of that matters if you're dead. The brain's highest priority is survival. So the question is, *What* has the brain had to protect us from? The table on page 7 gives an idea of what we humans have died from over the course of history, and the fates that your and my ancestors therefore had to escape.

Now, you may well be thinking, *What does all this have to do with me? I'm no hunter-gatherer.* Of course not, but your body and brain still think you are. Evolution is so slow that it tends to take tens, if not hundreds of thousands of years for major changes to appear within a species. This is also true of humans. The lifestyle that you and I are used to is no more than a flash in the pan of our history, and it has materialized over far too short a period of time for our bodies to have had time to adapt to it.

So, although the "work" field on your social media profile may say that you are a teacher, nursing assistant, systems developer, salesperson, plumber, taxi driver, journalist, chef or doctor, in purely biological terms it should say that you are a hunter-gatherer, as your body and brain haven't changed substantially in the past 10,000 or even 20,000 years. The single most important thing that we can learn about our species is how little we have actually changed. Our entire recorded history going back some 5,000 years—and at least twice as much again—is made up of people like you and me, who are in fact hunter-gatherers. So, what is this life that we have *actually* evolved to lead?

250,000 years in two minutes

It's easy to romanticize the hunter-gatherer way of life as a Huckleberry Finn existence filled with adventure and hunting expeditions, lived in small, close-knit communities in an unspoiled world. But, in actual fact, there is much to suggest that our ancestors' lives were in many ways complete hell. The average life expectancy was around 30 years, which isn't to say that everyone would drop dead at 30, but that many died young. As many as half died before they reached their teens—normally during birth or of an infection. Those who did make it to adulthood lived with the looming threat of starvation, blood loss, dehydration, animal attacks, even more infections, accidents and murder. Only a fraction would have made it to today's retirement age—and yes, there were hunter-gatherers who lived to be 70 or even 80. So old age per se is nothing new, but the fact that *so many* people are now reaching it is.

Around 10,000 years ago probably the single most significant shift in our ancestors' way of life occurred: we became farmers. But spears and bows weren't replaced by plows overnight; this gradual transition from a nomadic to an agricultural lifestyle took place over the course of centuries. The farmers' living conditions can be summarized quite simply: an even greater hell. The average life expectancy of around 30 years and the ever-present threat of death remained unchanged, albeit perhaps with a lesser risk of starvation. Instead, murder became an increasingly common cause of death, presumably because improved means of storing food and harvesting resources meant there was more to fight over. Hierarchies became more pronounced, and on top of that a number of contagious diseases appeared on the scene (more on this later). Work tasks grew more monotonous and working hours longer. Diets became less varied, most likely consisting of cereals for breakfast, lunch and dinner.

Prominent historians and thinkers have called the transition to an agrarian society humanity's greatest mistake. So why did we make that change if so much got worse? The main reason is probably that agriculture has the capacity to produce considerably more calories than hunting over the same area. And when you have mouths to feed, you don't have the luxury of complaining about the diet being unvaried, the job dull or someone else swiping a piece of what you have managed to scrape together.

More calories meant that more people could eat their fill, and when not everyone had to spend their days sourcing food, we could start specializing. Technological development took off, and our societies became ever more complex. All of this resulted in explosive population growth. Ten thousand years ago, before this shift to agriculture, there were 5 million people on earth. By 1850, before the Industrial Revolution, that figure was 1.2 billion: an increase of 24,000 percent over 400 generations!

But let's return to Eve, who I opened this chapter with, and tell her that in the future virtually every threat she knows will be eradicated. Her distant great-great-great-great- (etc.) grandchildren will live in a world in which deadly infectious diseases are not as common and almost no one need lose sleep over an animal attack. A world in which it is uncommon for a woman to die in childbirth. In which varied, energy-rich foods from every corner of the globe are available basically anywhere, and even boredom is a thing of the past.

Eve would probably think we were pulling her leg. But if we were able to convince her that her future descendants would boast all this, she would probably be delighted to know that her toil would one day reap such fantastic rewards. However, if we were then to tell her that one in eight people would be feeling so low that they needed medication, the term "medication" probably wouldn't be the only thing that she would struggle to understand. She might even think us ungrateful.

So, are we ungrateful in not seeing how good we have it? I can certainly feel ungrateful myself when I'm a little down for no reason. And I have lost count of the number of patients I have met who are ashamed to feel depressed or anxious despite their needs being met. But it isn't quite as simple as that. As mentioned, you and I are the children of the survivors, and perhaps feeling great just isn't the point.

I get that it may sound hopeless that our evolutionary history may make us genetically programmed to experience mental health problems, and that anxiety and angst have been key to our survival. But there are still things that we can do to feel better, which we will look at in more detail later on. First, we need to understand why we experience pleasure, worry, indifference, discomfort, joy, irritation, apathy and euphoria at all, when we could just as easily go around like robots. Indeed, why *do* we have feelings?

CHAPTER 2

WHY DO WE HAVE FEELINGS?

We are not thinking machines that feel, we are feeling machines that think.

ANTONIO DAMASIO, NEUROLOGIST AND WRITER

IMAGINE THAT YOU are rushing home from work. It's pouring down with rain and the sky is pitch black, but the November weather is not what's on your mind. You have at least two hours' work left to do tonight, but first you have to pick up your daughter from preschool before it closes. And pop by the supermarket. And get the laundry done. And tidy up because your in-laws are coming for dinner. And send off that job application. Come to think of it, shouldn't you . . . ?

When you go to cross the street outside work, your mind is somewhere else entirely.

Suddenly it's as though an invisible force makes you jump backward, just as a bus comes roaring past. You stand there, frozen on the edge of the curb, less than a foot away from having been run over. *Phew, that was close.* No one around you has noticed what just happened, but for you the whole world has stopped. The raindrops mix with your sweat as, pulse racing, you realize you just came within a hair's breadth of certain death. *That could have been it for me.* But luckily it wasn't, because something took control of you and snapped you out of your ponderings about deadlines, tidying up and cooking. Something commanded you to take a step back.

Your invisible helping hand is the size of an almond and sits deep within your temporal lobes. It is called the amygdala, and it has a hand in so many processes and has so many connections to other parts of the brain that it has been described as the brain's very own "godfather." One of the amygdala's most important tasks is to scan your surroundings for danger by processing the information being fed in by your senses. Sensory impressions relating to sight, sound, taste and smell actually go direct to the amygdala, which finds out what you are seeing, hearing, tasting and smelling before that information has been processed by the rest of the brain.

The brain is organized this way because it takes a few tenths of a second for visual information to be transported from the eye, via the optic nerve, to the different parts of the visual cortex in the occipital lobes. Only then do you finally become aware of what you are seeing. In critical situations, these few tenths of a second can be the difference between life and death. So, if the sensory impressions are serious enough, the amygdala can react before the rest of the brain— for example, when a bus is careering toward you. When the amygdala hits the alarm button, you step backward and stress hormones are released in your body. This is aptly called an *emotional* response, seeing as your step was of course a *motion*. Meanwhile, the subjective experience of fear that you feel when you realize you have narrowly escaped being run over is called a *feeling*. In summary: the emotion and motion come first, then comes the feeling. But let's take a closer look at what happens when the activation of the amygdala creates a feeling of terror inside you when you realize that you have had a very close shave.

A pooling of our outer and inner worlds

When we think about how the brain reacts to our environment, our physical surroundings are often what come to mind—such as a bus heading our way. But there is also another world that is at least as important here and that the brain monitors closely: our inner world. Deep inside your temporal lobe lies one of the most fascinating parts of the brain: the insula. The insula acts as a sort of compiling station, taking in information from the body such as heart rate, blood pressure, blood sugar level and breathing rate. It also receives the information coming from our senses. As a result, the insula is where our outer and inner worlds converge. And from this we get feelings!

In essence, feelings have just one purpose: to affect our behavior and, in doing so, to help us survive so that we can procreate.

Feelings don't simply wash over us in response to what's going on around us; they are *created* by the brain, which combines what's going on around us with what's going on *inside* us. Using this data, the brain tries to make us behave in a way that will ensure our survival. In essence, feelings have just one purpose: to affect our behavior and, in doing so, to help us survive so that we can procreate.

Automated intelligence

Every second, your eyes deliver at least 10 million bits of information to your brain. It's like a thick super-optic cable constantly spouting visual impressions. A number of equally thick cables also supply impressions from your hearing, taste and smell, on top of all the information coming in from every organ in your body. Your brain is positively swamped with information, and while its processing capacity is almost inconceivably efficient, a bottleneck does occur, and that is in your attention. You can only focus on one thing at a time and have *one* broad thought on your mind at a time. As a result, your brain does almost all its work without you knowing a thing about it and gives you a summary in the form of a feeling. We can liken our attention to the CEO of a major corporation. If the CEO asks a group of employees to review an important matter and they come back with 15 binders full of documents, the CEO will say: "I don't have time for this—summarize what you think I should do in half a page." Our feelings are one such summary, and they are there to guide our behavior.

YOUR BRAIN DOESN'T LOOK LIKE MINE

Just as our faces and bodies differ from each other's in appearance, so too do our brains. The insula is one of the parts of the brain that varies most in size from person to person. As the insula plays a key role in receiving signals from the body and turning them into feelings, a number of researchers believe that these size differences mean we experience signals from the body to different degrees. For some people, the volume dial for internal impressions will be turned up, and they will experience digestive discomfort, a heightened pulse or an aching back particularly keenly. For others, that volume dial will be turned down, and they will hardly notice these stimuli. Such differences in how strongly we react to our body's signals may come

---

down in part to the differences in size between different people's insulae.

There is also fascinating research underway into whether differences in the size and activity of the insula can be linked to personality. For example, neuroticism—a personality trait that affects how strongly individuals react to negative impressions—would appear to be linked to activity in the insula. That differences in the size and activity of the insula have a role to play in different personality traits and how strongly we react to our body's signals may fool us into thinking that there is such a thing as a "normal" insula. There is no such thing, in the same way that there is no such thing as a "normal" brain. In fact, in gregarious creatures like humans, our brains are *supposed* to be different. Having different traits and feelings represented within a herd was most likely crucial to our survival.

From banana tree to kitchen counter

The brain doesn't just create feelings to guide our behavior when pulling us out of the way of an approaching bus; it creates them in every waking moment of our lives. Let's take a less dramatic example. You have just stepped into your kitchen. On the counter lies a banana, and you consider whether or not to eat it. How does the brain make such a routine decision? Well, first it needs to gauge the energy and nutritional value of the banana. Then it has to gather information on the nutrient reserves in your body and whether they need topping up—and whether a banana is what your body actually needs.

Now, if we had to consciously run these sums every time we considered having a bite to eat, it would get pretty old pretty fast. So your brain does the job for you without you knowing anything about it. It weighs up all the factors and comes up with an answer, and this is where your feelings come into play. The answer is delivered to you in the form of a feeling: you feel hungry and eat the banana, or feel full and skip it.

But if Eve, who we met at the start of this book, was faced with the decision of whether to *climb* a banana tree, she would have to weigh up a myriad of additional factors: the number of bananas in the tree, their size and ripeness, whether her nutrient reserves were replete or she was in desperate need of food, and her physical capability to climb the tree. She would also have to consider the risks, such as how high up the bananas were, or if the tree looked hard to climb, or if there were predators in the area.

Obviously, Eve didn't whip out a pen and paper (even less an Excel spreadsheet) to make her calculations; she did exactly what you do in your kitchen. Her brain made a calculation and delivered a decision in the form of a feeling. If the risk of getting hurt was small and the tree was full of fruit, or her energy needs were great, she would feel brave and decide to start climbing. But if the risks were significant, the prize small or her energy reserves full, the answer would come as a feeling of fear or fullness, and she would leave the bananas untouched.

Although this calculation is essentially the same whether you're in the kitchen or at the foot of a tree, there is one crucial difference: it doesn't matter if your kitchen calculation is wrong, because if you decide not to eat the banana, you can always come back for it later on. Eve, however, didn't have that luxury. If her calculations were skewed in favor of consistently throwing caution to the wind, her recklessness would sooner or later risk killing her. Conversely, if her calculations were skewed in favor of never taking any chances, her extreme caution would instead risk her starving to death. Only those of our ancestors whose feelings gave them the right guidance—and by "right" I mean favoring survival and reproduction—were able to survive and pass on their genes. And so it went on, generation after generation. Millennium after millennium.

As we can see, feelings aren't vague phenomena that we would be better off without. They are created by the brain in order to guide our behavior, and they have been honed over millions of years by evolution's ruthless selection. The feelings that nudged us toward the "wrong" behaviors—again, "wrong" from a survival standpoint—have left our gene pool for the simple reason that none of the people who had those feelings lasted. Biologically speaking, feelings are billions of brain cells exchanging biochemical substances that nudge us toward behaviors that promote survival and reproduction. Or, more poetically, feelings are whispers from the thousands of generations past who managed, against all odds, to elude starvation, infectious disease and sudden death.

Why happily is never ever after

What I have just described helps us to understand why we can't feel great all the time. Let's say Eve did decide to climb that tree and managed to get her hands on some bananas. Satisfied, she sat down and tucked in. But for how long could she afford to feel satisfied? As it happens, not all that long. Had her satisfaction from that effort lasted a matter of months, she would have had no motivation to seek out more food and would have soon starved to death.

This means that feelings of well-being are *supposed* to be fleeting, as otherwise they would be unfit for purpose—i.e., for motivating us. Most of us will of course know this feeling all too well. We think that if we could just get this or that promotion at work, a new car, a bigger pay package or a perfect bathroom, we would be happy with our lot. But should any or all of that actually happen, it turns out that the feeling is quickly replaced by a new longing for an even better promotion or an even bigger pay raise. As we know, it never ends!

"Well-being" often tends to rank highly in lists of what we think matters most in life. But this state is just one of many tools in our evolutionary toolbox. And as a tool, it's ineffective if it isn't fleeting. Therefore, expecting to always feel great is about as unrealistic as expecting that banana on the kitchen counter to keep you full for the rest of your life. We just aren't built that way.

However, when we lift the lid and take a look inside our brains, feelings aren't the only things that work differently than how we might imagine. Psychological and neuroscientific research has revealed that the brain alters our memories. It turns a blind eye to inconvenient truths to help us belong to a group. It often fools us into thinking that we are better, more competent and more outgoing than we really are—and even into thinking that we are worthless, too. The brain doesn't let us experience the world as it really is; it has a much more important, and much narrower, task at hand: survival. As a result, it shows us the world as we have *had* to see it in order to survive. Which leads us to our greatest emotional blight: anxiety.

CHAPTER 3

ANXIETY AND PANIC

I've lived through some terrible things in my life,
some of which actually happened.

MARK TWAIN

YOU HAVE DEFINITELY experienced anxiety before. How can
I be so sure? Because it's just as natural a part of our biology as hunger and fatigue. Anxiety is an intense sense of discomfort—the sense
that something is wrong. To quote one very wise patient, anxiety
feels like "wanting to crawl out of your own skin." When someone
says that they are not feeling well mentally, they are most likely experiencing anxiety.

We experience anxiety to different extents and in different forms.
Some people suffer from constant, low-level anxiety, as though there
is always something preventing them from feeling completely at ease.
For others the anxiety might be sudden and intense. For some it could
be linked to something specific, such as public speaking, while others
will see an array of more or less likely catastrophes playing out before
them, such as the plane they are on crashing, their children being kid-
napped or them getting fired and having to sell the family home.

The best way to describe anxiety is as a sort of "preemptive stress." If your boss lashes out at you at work, then naturally you will feel stressed. But if you think: *What if my boss yells at me at work?* then that's anxiety. The reactions in our brains and bodies are basically the same, but the difference is that stress is triggered by a threat, while anxiety is triggered by the thought of a *potential* threat. In practice, there are just as many forms of anxiety as there are people, but when it comes down to it, any anxiety is the brain's way of telling us that something is wrong—and thereby activating the stress system. This "something" can be both vague and unrealistic. Apparently, the brain just loves to tell us that something is wrong.

"Something in me must be broken"

A 26-year-old man stepped into my practice and recounted the following:

> I'd slept badly and was stressed about an important meeting at work. When I stepped onto the subway at just after eight, I'd hoped for a seat so I could take one last look at some important documents, but the train was rammed. In the tunnel between two stops the train suddenly ground to a halt and all the lights went out. I was gripped by sheer panic, beyond anything I've ever felt before. My heart was pounding and my mind was racing, and it was like this shell formed around me. I felt a pain in my chest and was gasping for air. I just wanted out of that dark, stationary, confined carriage. As I crouched down, all I could think was that I was having a heart attack and was going to die.
>
> The people were staring; a few pointed and whispered. The ones closest to me started edging away. A kindly older lady bent down and asked me what the matter was, but I

couldn't even reply. Funnily enough, I did manage to think how tragic it was that my life was going to end in a subway car, of all places.

By the time the train finally started moving again, someone had called me an ambulance, which met me at the next station. Three hours later I was sitting in the emergency room, awaiting test results. According to the doctor, it hadn't been a heart attack—my ECG and blood tests were normal—but a panic attack. She asked me how I was really feeling, and suggested I see a psychiatrist. I asked her to check the ECG again—there had to be some kind of mistake. But she said there was no question of any mistake and that she'd met lots of people in my situation.

When I met this man one week later, he told me that, yes, he had been feeling quite stressed lately, due to deadlines and a faltering relationship. But he couldn't understand why that would create such sudden, debilitating anxiety. And why on the subway? For him it was a sign that something inside him had cracked.

Roughly one in four of us will experience a panic attack—the most intense form of anxiety—at some point in our lives. Panic attacks are an extremely acute sense of discomfort and are often accompanied by a racing heart, shortness of breath and a debilitating perceived loss of control. Between 3 and 5 percent of people will suffer repeated panic attacks and limit their lives as a result. They avoid subways, buses and confined or open spaces. The so-called "anticipatory anxiety" linked to attacks can cause just as much suffering as the attacks themselves.

During a first panic attack, many people go to the hospital convinced that they are having a heart attack. Once we doctors have established that it is in fact a panic attack, our first course of action is to reassure the patient that they aren't in any danger. Their heart won't stop beating and they won't stop breathing, even if that's the way it feels. Most people with severe anxiety are completely certain that there's something seriously wrong with them. So let's take a closer look at what really happens in the body and brain during a panic attack.

There is much to suggest that the attack originates in the amygdala, which I described in the previous chapter, and which, among other things, is tasked with seeking out danger in our environment. The amygdala flags a possible hazard and the body reacts by jumping into fight-or-flight mode. In turn, the stress system gears up, increasing the pulse and breathing rate. The brain then misinterprets these signals from the body as proof that there really is an imminent danger and ups the ante even more. The pulse and breathing rate rise even farther, which the brain misinterprets as even stronger proof that something dangerous is afoot. At which point we are spiraling toward full-blown panic.

The smoke detector principle

You may think that this vicious cycle of misinterpretations ought to mean that there's a glitch in the brain, but let's now take a look at my patient's reaction from an evolutionary biological perspective. You see, the engine of a panic attack, the amygdala, is fast but sloppy. The amygdala works by what we call "the smoke detector principle." If the smoke detector in our kitchen were to go off unnecessarily— for example, from burnt toast—we could accept this as long as we were certain that it would go off if there really was a fire. The amygdala works in exactly the same way—it tends to go off one time too many to make sure it never misses an actual hazard. But what does "one time too many" mean in practice? The American psychiatrist

Randolph Nesse explains it using the following example: let's say you are in the savanna and hear a rustling in the bushes. Now, this noise is probably just the wind, but there's a small chance it could be a lion. If you fly off in a panic, it will cost you roughly 100 calories: that's what your body will burn by running away, so it's what you stand to lose in energy if the rustling really is just the wind. However, if your brain *doesn't* activate the stress system and it is in fact a lion, that will cost you 100,000 calories: what the lion will get from eating you.

By this crude calorie logic, the brain should activate the stress system 1,000 times more often than is called for. You may smirk at such an artificial example, but it does give an idea of what it means to have inner warning systems that were calibrated over hundreds of thousands of years, in a much more dangerous world. People who saw dangers all around them, and who constantly planned for disaster upon disaster, had a greater chance of survival than those who kicked back and relaxed by the campfire. This tendency to see danger at every turn and constantly plan for disasters is what we now call anxiety. And the body activating the stress system so forcefully that you feel the overwhelming urge to run away is what we now call a panic attack.

In summary, each individual anxiety attack doesn't actually have to fulfill a function in and of itself. That just a fraction of all panic attacks at some point saved our lives was enough for the brain to calibrate itself to err on the side of caution. From the brain's perspective, we can therefore see a panic attack as a false alarm and a sign that it's doing exactly what it's supposed to do, in much the same way that a smoke detector that tells us our toast is burnt is also showing us that it's doing its job. The fact that our stress system would rather kick into action one time too many than one time too few does indeed serve a purpose and is no glitch.

But if a hypersensitive stress system helped us to survive, you may wonder why we don't fly off in a panic at the slightest little thing. How can anyone so much as step inside a subway car without getting a panic attack? Shouldn't those of our ancestors who were extremely cautious have had the best chances of avoiding the lion's clutches, the snake's venom and the fatal rockslide? But the reason that we aren't all constantly on edge all the time is that in nature everything is a compromise, and everything comes at a cost. A giraffe's long neck and legs may help it to reach leaves that other animals can't get at, but if those legs get *too* long, they risk breaking. A slim antelope may run fast, but without fat stores it has no reserves to dip into when food is scarce. Had our ancestors seen danger at every turn, their risk of dying in an accident or predator attack would indeed have been smaller. But had they perceived *everything* as life-threatening and jumped at their own shadow, they would never have been able to summon the courage required to find food or a mate. In other words, favorable qualities almost always come at a cost.

Now, you may argue that *all* panic attacks on the subway are by definition dysfunctional, as they fulfill no function. This is of course true, but instead of considering their function by today's standards, we should really be asking ourselves what historical situations may have demanded such a reaction. Were such situations common? From a survival standpoint, could it have been beneficial to us to be able to get away from somewhere at any cost? The answer to these questions is likely yes. Which is why we should neither be surprised that our defense mechanisms can have serious consequences—such as panic attacks on the subway—nor that these mechanisms spring into action so readily—better "one time too many" than "one time too few."

In summary, the main reason why we still get anxiety in spite of our secure lives is that the brain's alarm system is still tailored to a world in which half the population died before they reached their teens. A world in which the ability to see danger at every conceivable—and inconceivable—turn improved the chances of survival. You and I are the descendants of these survivors, and as our susceptibility to anxiety is around 40 percent determined by genes (yes, this is a real figure), then the vast majority of people will perceive the world as being more dangerous than it is.

Given all this, it isn't strange that some people have anxiety. What's stranger is that there are people who *don't*! Strong arms can lift great weights and strong legs can run fast, but a strong brain isn't immune to stress, adversity and loneliness; rather, it does whatever it can to get us through. Sometimes this involves generating feelings of worry, or making us want to withdraw or view the world as dangerous. If we believe that these symptoms mean the brain is faulty or sick, then we have forgotten that the brain's most important function is survival. Had our ancestors' anxiety been less easily piqued, you and I simply wouldn't be here today. Now, imagine if everyone knew this. Just like my patient in the subway car, many people who live with anxiety are convinced there's something wrong with them. When they realize anxiety can actually be a sign that their brain is working the way it's supposed to, it can come as a relief.

Strong arms can lift great weights, but a strong brain isn't immune to stress; rather, it does whatever it can to get us through.

Much later, the patient who had a panic attack on the subway told me that when he realized that a panic attack is a false alarm that shows that the brain is working the way it is supposed to, he accepted that it's OK to have them. And when he realized that—the attacks started happening less frequently! Another patient described how much it calmed her to think: *It's just my amygdala wanting me to be afraid.* When viewed from this perspective, it isn't only panic attacks that become more understandable; post-traumatic stress disorder (PTSD) does, too.

HISTORIC THREATS

Perhaps you are still skeptical as to whether your anxiety has anything to do with your evolutionary heritage. In that case, we can turn our attention to what gives us phobias—that is to say, disproportionately intense fears. The most common phobias are public speaking, heights, confined spaces, open expanses, snakes and spiders. And what do all of these have in common? The fact that virtually no one dies of any of these anymore, but that they all posed a threat to us historically.

Take snakebites, which kill on average four people in Europe each year. Compare this to road accidents, which cause roughly 80,000 deaths in Europe and over 1.3 million deaths worldwide annually. In theory, no one should really be afraid of snakes—but the mere sight of a car should give us the heebie-jeebies.

Or take public speaking. It's highly unlikely that a muddled speech at a 50th birthday party or a faltering presentation at school or work will cost you your life. Meanwhile, each year, smoking takes the lives of 7 million people, and physical inactivity leads to 5 million early deaths. So why do so many of us have a minor breakdown at the thought of speaking in front of others, but shrug at cigarettes and comfy sofas? The answer is that physical inactivity and smoking never posed us a threat historically, and as a result we haven't developed a fear of them. Public speaking, on the other hand, used to bring with it the risk of exclusion, which for almost all previous generations of humans would have been equivalent to mortal danger. Belonging to a group was basically as important as having food, and as a consequence the brain interprets public speaking as a potential threat to our life. The fact that snakes and public speaking still elicit such strong fears in many of us is one of the clearest signs we have that our susceptibility to anxiety was shaped in another world.

Harrowing memories

In the summer of 2005 I was working as a junior doctor in an emergency psychiatric unit. One of my patients was a woman in her early fifties who had been on a family vacation in Thailand seven months earlier when the catastrophic tsunami struck. They had been staying at a hotel on high ground so were out of danger, but being a nurse she went to a local hospital to offer her help. There she came to witness harrowing scenes involving seriously wounded or dead patients, many of whom were children.

Back home, she had initially felt uneasy, but life soon returned to normal. However, after a few months she started getting nightmares about her and her children drowning, and they would be so upsetting that she would be hesitant to go to bed. By day she would be overcome by awful flashbacks to the Thai hospital. As a result, she started doing whatever she could to escape any reminder of the trip. She canceled her daily newspaper subscription and stopped watching the news. But that wasn't enough. Simply setting foot on the same street as the police station where she had renewed her passport gave her severe anxiety. Gradually she started avoiding more and more places, and she felt her life was shrinking before her eyes. "It's like I've lost control of my life, like I'm not calling the shots anymore," she said.

It was clear that she was suffering from PTSD, a particularly severe form of anxiety that often involves painful memories of a disturbing event that the sufferer has experienced or witnessed. In waking hours these memories appear as so-called flashbacks; in sleep, in the form of nightmares. Those affected are constantly on edge and avoid anything that might trigger even the slightest reminder of the incident.

PTSD was first studied in soldiers returning from war. The symptoms of flashbacks, nightmares and hypervigilance have, of course, been the same for soldiers of all wars, but the name of the diagnosis has changed. Veterans of WWI and WWII were diagnosed with "shell shock" or "war neurosis." The term "PTSD" only came into public awareness during the Vietnam War.

We now know that PTSD affects up to one-third of soldiers who return from combat, but you don't have to have experienced war or a natural disaster to get PTSD; traumatic experiences such as abuse, bullying or sexual assault can have a similar effect. The same is true for those who have been exposed to or witnessed violence in the home.

Being traumatized means that the brain believes the trauma is still continuing, and this was clearly the case for my patient. It may seem like a cruel trick of nature that, day and night, her brain kept her on her guard by repeatedly reliving those disturbing events. What's the point of reminding yourself of something that happened seven months ago on the other side of the world? To understand this, we need to take a closer look at what memory really is.

Memory: a guide to the future

In the previous chapter we saw that our feelings developed to help us survive. The same is true of our ability to remember: we remember in order to survive, not to reminisce. In fact, our memories have nothing to do with the past; they are our brains' aids for the here and

THE HAPPINESS CURE

now. In every moment of your life, your brain is pulling up memories to guide you, which it does by selecting the ones it considers most relevant to, or reminiscent of, what you are experiencing right now. Therefore, last year's Christmas may feel very recent when you look back on it during the festive season, but distant if you think about it in summer.

While it's true that the brain has an unfathomable capacity for memory, it can't recall everything that we experience; we would be far too slow on the uptake if we were constantly having to trawl back through every moment of our lives. So the brain chooses what to remember, and it makes many of these decisions while we are asleep. In our sleep, it sifts through the day's events and selects what is to be saved, as memories, or discarded and forgotten. This choice is far from arbitrary. The brain prioritizes memories that it considers important to our survival, particularly those linked to threat and danger.

The amygdala—that small, almond-shaped region tasked with, among other things, alerting us to possible danger—is situated right in front of the hippocampus, the brain's memory center. This anatomical proximity reflects how closely bound powerful emotional experiences and memory are. When we have what we feel is an emotionally intense experience, it's a sign that that experience is somehow important to our survival and should therefore be prioritized by the brain. If the amygdala is activated—for example, in the face of a threat—the hippocampus receives a signal to take note of what we are currently experiencing, and creates a memory in crisp, high definition. Seven months after the tsunami, my patient still remembered the events as though they had happened yesterday. These memories were made to be easily triggered, even by stimuli with only the most tenuous of links to the event in question—such as the street where my patient collected her passport before the trip.

There is nothing wrong with a brain that creates clear, easily retrievable memories of traumatic experiences. After all, the brain's primary mission is to ensure our survival, even in the most testing of circumstances. As a result, it does all it can to prevent us from ending up in a similarly life-threatening situation. And if in spite of these efforts we end up in the same situation again, it will ensure we have a razor-sharp image at hand of how we overcame it last time. It may seem bizarre that painful memories of Thailand could be reawakened by a street at home, where the threat of drowning in a tidal wave is pretty much nil, but if the brain rings that alarm bell, it's simply because it hasn't adapted to the fact that we can jet off to faraway lands some 5,000 miles away.

Anything that might bear even the slightest resemblance to a previous traumatic experience will make the brain pull up that memory for our protection, and as a result the memories that the brain considers most important to store are often those that we would rather forget. This applies to all of us, not just those who suffer from PTSD. Perhaps you have a painful memory that pops up every now and then; this is your brain's way of trying to prevent the same thing from happening again. By reliving the memory over and over, it reminds you of how you handled it last time. That these reminders have an impact on our mental health is of secondary importance to the brain, which is, as we know, designed for survival rather than well-being.

The biology behind "talking about it"

Of course, it will come as cold comfort to those who suffer from PTSD that painful memories are in fact misguided kindness from an overprotective brain. Still, considering the brain's perspective not only gives us an understanding of what PTSD really is; it also provides us with an important key to alleviating and treating the condition. For, as it happens, whenever we pull up a memory, it becomes unstable and therefore malleable. In effect, our memories change when we think about them.

It may sound whimsical to suggest that memories can change. After all, we tend to view them as YouTube clips that we can pull up, watch and put away, safe in the knowledge that we'll see exactly the same clip when we pull them up again later. However, psychological research has revealed that our memories are more like Wikipedia pages, which are subject to constant updates and edits. These updates tend to happen when we pull them up—i.e., think about them.

Let's take an example. Cast your mind back to your very first day of school. Perhaps you're picturing a teacher standing in front of a blackboard, or a classroom decked out for autumn, or your classmates dressed up nicely. Perhaps you can even recall the scent of birch twigs on the air, or feel that buzz of excitement and anticipation. In the now, as you are casting your mind back, your memories of your first school day are actually changing slightly—but the shape that these changes take will depend on what you are experiencing and feeling right now. In other words, these memories will be tinted by your current state of mind. If you are feeling happy, they will become slightly more positive; if you are feeling down, they will become slightly more negative.

Why our memories work in this way is easily understood if we spotlight the fact that their primary task is to help us survive—not to give an objective rendering of our experiences. Let's say you experience a bear attack one day while walking in the forest and only narrowly manage to escape. Your brain will create a sharp, easily retrievable memory of the attack to prevent you from ever returning to the same spot, or, failing that, to make you extremely vigilant and ready to react if you do. But let's imagine now that you do return to the same spot and this time there's no bear to be found. And there's no bear again the next time. Or the time after that. By now the original memory of that spot will have started to shift from being extremely threatening to slightly less so. The brain updates your memory so that it's better aligned with the appropriate level of fear. After all, if you have walked the same route through the forest a hundred times and only met a bear on one of those occasions, the odds are fairly slim that you'd encounter one on walk number 101.

It follows that what we normally perceive as a "good" memory— i.e., an exact rendering of what happened—isn't necessarily desirable from the brain's perspective. Memories are, and should be, plastic, and to give us the best possible guidance they should be updated based on the context in which they are accessed.

All of this can be put to good use in the treatment of PTSD. By airing unpleasant memories in an environment in which we feel safe, they will gradually start to feel less threatening. So do talk about them, but do so in an environment in which you feel calm and safe, either with close friends or with a therapist. And tread carefully. If the memories are particularly painful, a good first step may be to write them down.

Airing painful memories in a safe environment—whether it's a memory of an accident, bullying, harassment or abuse—fulfills the same function as returning to that route through the forest and not meeting a bear. Slowly but surely the memory will become less threatening. Neurologically speaking, trying to suppress traumatic memories is often a bad strategy, because it means they never change. They become set in stone.

Panic attacks and PTSD—arguably the most painful forms of anxiety—are the brain's way of trying to protect you. The same is true of all forms of anxiety: the brain wants you to be cautious and to put safety first. Which leads us to the main thing we need to know about anxiety: it isn't dangerous. This in no way suggests it should be trivialized—quite the opposite. For the person affected, anxiety can be extremely painful. Anyone who has experienced severe anxiety—whatever the form—will know that it has the capacity to take over and poison an entire life. Trying to wish severe anxiety away is like trying to change the direction of a storm by blowing into the prevailing wind: it won't work.

We all know that it's extremely unlikely that a plane will crash, or that we will suffocate in a confined subway car, but that makes no difference to us in the moment: the anxiety steamrolls any logical counterargument, making it impossible to think of anything else. And that's the whole point! If we could simply shake off anxiety with platitudes like "Choose joy, not fear!" or "Think positive!" it would never have existed in the first place. If it were possible to wrong-foot it so easily, it would have been too flimsy a means of influencing our behavior.

When should I seek help?

Virtually everyone is affected by anxiety at some point, but where do we draw the line between what is "normal" and when we should seek help? A good rule of thumb is to seek help if the anxiety is life-limiting. If there is something that you'd like to do (rather than *are expected* to do) but have been avoiding due to intense discomfort— be that going to a party, to a networking event, to the movie theater or traveling—then I think you should seek help for it.

When we feel discomfort at the prospect of doing something, we tend to avoid it completely, which is the very pattern that therapy for anxiety disorders tries to break. By exposing yourself in a slow and con-trolled way to whatever it is that gives you anxiety, your brain learns that its smoke detector may be slightly overactive, and so it may become less sensitive. By talking about harrowing memories we reshape them, but this takes time. After all, we are configured to flee a thousand rus-tling bushes to avoid a single lion. To overcome a fear of public speaking, it isn't enough to do it two or three times. It takes consider-ably more than that but, with time, practice usually reaps rewards.

The basis of almost all therapy for anxiety disorders is the understanding that we perceive the world as more dangerous and threatening than it really is, and that we should pay less attention to those thoughts. But it's one thing to read that and quite another to put it into practice. One strategy that has really helped some of my patients to shut out those thoughts is to see anxiety from the brain's perspective. The brain isn't supposed to show us reality as it is, but rather as we need to see it in order to survive. When our brain views the world as dark and threatening, it doesn't mean our constitution is "weak"; it means that we have a powerful brain that's doing exactly what it was meant to do.

Most people who do therapy get better. As a psychiatrist with an interest in evolutionary biology, I have complete respect for how powerful anxiety can and indeed *should* be in order to serve its purpose. Still, I never cease to be amazed by the brain's fantastic capacity for change when I see the effect that therapy—in particular cognitive behavioral therapy—can have on my patients. But therapy isn't the only thing that works. One overlooked and surprisingly effective treatment for almost all forms of anxiety is physical activity—which also has a long list of other positive side effects. Remember to start slowly, as intense physical activity leads to an increased pulse, which can be misinterpreted by the brain as imminent danger and instead lead to further anxiety. We'll take a closer look at managing anxiety through physical activity later on in this book. Many people with severe anxiety also find antidepressant medication helpful, so if you suffer from a severe anxiety disorder, do consider speaking to your doctor about this.

Different treatment methods are not mutually exclusive and, interestingly enough, seem to affect different parts of the brain. It appears that physical activity and medication allay the alarm systems in the deeper regions of the brain, such as the amygdala. Therapy, on the other hand, puts the most advanced parts of the brain to use, such as our frontal lobes, and teaches us how to mentally manage anxiety when it does crop up. For most people, a combination of several methods works best. When it comes to treating anxiety, one plus one can often equal four or five, so the more fronts we tackle it on, the better.

TWO BRAIN TRICKS TO COMBAT ANXIETY

1. **BREATHING.** If you are experiencing acute anxiety, one solid tip can be to focus on your breaths. By breathing calmly, with long exhales, the body sends signals to the brain that there is no danger. You see, the part of the nervous system that governs how our organs work lies outside of our mind's control. This system is called the autonomic nervous system and it consists of two distinct parts: the sympathetic nervous system, which is often linked to our fight-or-flight response, and the parasympathetic nervous system, which is associated with digestion and rest.

Our breathing affects the interplay between the sympathetic and parasympathetic nervous systems. When we inhale, the activity of the sympathetic nervous system increases slightly, nudging us toward a fight-or-flight response. In fact, the heart beats slightly faster on an inhale, so it's no coincidence that athletes take a few sharp breaths to pump themselves up for a race: by doing this they are activating their fight-or-flight response. Conversely, when we exhale, the activity of the parasympathetic nervous system increases. The heart beats slightly more slowly and the fight-or-flight response is dampened.

So if you feel anxiety coming on, you can step aside for a few minutes and take a few calm, deep breaths, taking particular care to make the exhale longer than the inhale. As a rule of thumb, aim to breathe in for four seconds and out for six. This is longer than feels natural, so practice it a few times to get a feel for it. Deep breaths with long exhales are a surprisingly effective way to "hack" the brain to regulate our fight-or-flight response. For many, the feeling of the anxiety trickling away that comes from doing this is palpable.

2. PUT IT INTO WORDS. If slow breathing doesn't help, there's another trick at hand: describe and articulate what you are feeling. Let me explain.

The frontal lobe (we actually have two, the medial and the lateral, one in each hemisphere of the brain) sits right behind the forehead and is the most advanced part of the brain. In very general terms, the medial part is between the eyes, and the lateral part is out by the temples.

The medial part is focused on the self. It registers what is going on inside the body and is important for feelings and motivation. The lateral part is the last area of the brain to mature, and it focuses on what is going on around us. This part is important in planning and problem-solving. If you place your finger between your eyebrows, you will be pointing at the part of the brain that turns the spotlight on yourself. Move your finger toward the outer edge of your eyebrow, however, and you will be moving toward the part that deals with what's going on in your surroundings.

Interestingly enough, the activation of the frontal lobe has a powerful dampening effect on the amygdala. When participants in an experiment were shown images of angry and scared faces, their amygdalae were activated. This comes as no real surprise: an angry person is a threat, after all, and a scared person may mean there's something we need to look out for nearby. However, when participants were asked to *articulate* what they saw—"She looks angry," "He looks scared"—the activity in their frontal lobes increased, particularly in the lateral areas. Studies have shown that the lateral part of the frontal lobe—i.e., the part that focuses on our surroundings—is activated when we describe how we feel. And since this activity dampens the amygdala, we can put it to good use to regulate our feelings.

Practice putting your feelings into words and try to make them as nuanced as possible. The better you get at articulating your feelings, the better you will be at observing them objectively rather than trailing in their wake.

From childhood trauma to defense mechanism

When I was growing up, mental illness was rarely discussed. I tended to associate the word "psychiatry" with straitjackets and padded rooms, while "anxiety" was a woolly term I lacked any real knowledge of, and which mainly called to mind the films of Ingmar Bergman. Today you can find 60,000 books on anxiety on Amazon, and a Google search of the same term brings up some 1.6 billion hits. This may fool us into thinking that anxiety is something new, but of course that isn't the case. Even the philosophers Epicurus (fourth century BCE), Cicero (around 50 BCE) and Seneca (around 50 CE) described the experience of anxiety. The latter two also offer tips on treatment, in what must be the world's first cognitive behavioral therapy manuals! So anxiety has been around for as long as we have. What's changed, however, is how we view it.

Anxiety was long regarded as the pitfall of foresight. The more possible scenarios we are able to imagine, the more we can worry about those we would rather avoid. Our advanced brains allow us to envisage a plethora of possible future outcomes, and to understand how our actions might lead to different ones. And while this does help us to plan, it can also be a source of anxiety, as it brings to mind even the possibilities that we wouldn't like to come to pass. Hence anxiety can be seen as the price we humans pay for our intelligence.

In the early twentieth century, however, Austrian psychiatrist Sigmund Freud put forward another theory. He believed that anxiety is often the result of unpleasant childhood memories that we have repressed. Freud viewed the human psyche as a battlefield, with the different parts of our subconscious fighting either to conceal painful memories or to bring them to light. Anxiety, Freud asserted, was the result of this inner conflict. If we could only identify and process those painful, repressed memories, he argued, our inner conflicts would resolve and our anxiety would disappear.

Let's try another experiment to explore this idea. Let's say I— ever an anxious soul—sought help at Freud's clinic in 1920s Vienna. Having positioned me on his analyst's couch and ponderously stroked his white beard, Freud would have asked me to recount my most traumatic childhood memory. To which I would have replied that I don't have any particularly traumatic childhood memories and that I had a generally happy upbringing.

"That's where you're mistaken!" Freud would have claimed. "Your neurotic disposition stems from past horrors that you have repressed. Spend enough time on my couch and we'll eventually root out some unresolved trauma that you have swept under the carpet, and then we can process it together. Perhaps we'll learn that your parents lost you on a beach or spanked you when you didn't clean your room. Something is bound to emerge, you mark my words!"

Now, Freud certainly made a valuable contribution to us starting to air our innermost feelings, but in the light of current research his ideas on anxiety come across as rather absurd. Fewer and fewer people take them seriously, which is a good thing in my book, as they often meant that parents would be blamed for their children's anxiety disorders. Of course, there's no question that a difficult childhood increases the risk of being affected by anxiety. When we experience intense stress in our early years, it signals to the brain that the world we live in is dangerous, which in turn makes the brain dial up its alarm systems and sensitivity to any "smoke." However, neither neuroscientific nor psychological research has turned up any support for the idea that anxiety is caused by *repressed* childhood memories. In fact, it has revealed that our predisposition to anxiety is almost 40 percent determined by genes. In other words, a large part of our susceptibility to developing anxiety has already been determined when we are born.

The reason for this detour to question Freud is that his impact was huge, and not only among psychologists and psychiatrists. Freud influenced writers, artists and directors, including the artist Salvador Dalí and directors Stanley Kubrick and Alfred Hitchcock, to name but a few. Through these cultural icons, Freud's ideas gained so much traction in wider society that his impact on our perceptions of our own psyche is almost impossible to overstate. It's important to recognize Freud's theories as they came to reshape our views on anxiety, taking it from a normal facet of life to something sickly that must be cured.

A stance more in line with current knowledge is that anxiety is a natural defense mechanism that protects us against dangers, and that it is often a sign that we are functioning entirely normally. Some people have a particularly keen defense mechanism and experience more anxiety than others—I personally belong to this group. Meanwhile, others whose defense mechanisms aren't so strong experience less anxiety. But what almost all of us have in common is that we experience more anxiety than we should.

Freud's theories about anxiety may have perhaps sounded insightful once, but they were no more than mere guesses. So why did they appeal to so many people? Perhaps because Freud gave us hope that we could free ourselves of anxiety entirely. That is, of course, a lovely thought, but as you have probably realized by this point, it's one that isn't particularly realistic in light of how we have evolved.

If you suffer from anxiety, I hope you don't feel that this chapter in any way trivializes or belittles your experience. As a psychiatrist I have seen far too many times how devastating anxiety can be for people and the enormous suffering it can bring. However, I have noticed that a biological view on anxiety can help people to see it from a broader perspective. Some of my patients have found it reassuring to think: *It's just my amygdala acting up* or *A panic attack is a false alarm and a sign that I'm functioning normally.* It makes their anxiety feel less chaotic and unpredictable. Some even find a logic in it—it feels more understandable, more normal. Not only is it reassuring to know that our inner chaos has both a purpose and a structure; it also gives us a spectator's seat from which we can observe our emotional lives. Almost all therapy—from cognitive behavioral therapy to psychodynamic therapy—involves getting used to observing our own emotions from the outside, and in my experience viewing anxiety from the brain's perspective can serve the same purpose. It works as a sort of therapy, allowing us to take a step back and observe our own feelings.

When patients describe how reassuring it can be to view their anxiety from the brain's perspective, it sometimes reminds me of one of the final scenes in the film *The Wizard of Oz.* In the scene, the protagonist Dorothy comes face to face with a terrifying wizard—until, that is, Dorothy's dog pulls back the curtain around him, and Dorothy realizes that what she has been fearing is not a wizard but a harmless phoney tugging levers and pressing buttons. The same is true of anxiety. Once we understand that anxiety isn't dangerous, and we know more about the neurobiological buttons the brain is pressing, it can feel that bit less threatening. Often, the more we learn about anxiety, the less it troubles us. And the more we learn, the kinder we are to ourselves. I have found that, for many, it gives them greater compassion for themselves.

That being said, if your anxiety is causing you harm, you should seek help. There is absolutely no intrinsic value to having anxiety or feeling unwell. But remember: anxiety is a natural part of life, and it was a condition of our survival. Anyone who expects to lead a life free of any anxiety will be disappointed; the vast majority of us just aren't built that way. But that doesn't mean that we're broken.

CHAPTER 4

DEPRESSION

Nothing makes sense in biology except in the light of evolution.

THEODOSIUS DOBZHANSKY, GENETICIST AND
EVOLUTIONARY BIOLOGIST

NOW THAT WE have examined anxiety from the brain's perspective, it's time that we turned our attention to our next major psychiatric diagnosis: depression. If you are a woman, there is a one in four chance that you will experience depression at some point in your life; if you are a man, that chance is one in seven. The World Health Organization estimates that over 280 million people have depression, making it the third greatest cause of ill health in the world. But despite the single, broad label we give this condition, not all 280 million people who have depression are experiencing the same thing.

The term "depression" comprises a wide spectrum of experiences, but the common denominators are feelings of sadness and a loss of interest in the activities one once enjoyed. Parties, holidays, hearing from friends—*everything* feels meaningless. And these feelings don't just last a day—we all have those days—but for weeks and months on end. The opposite of depression isn't so much happiness as vitality; depression feels like you are standing still, in a sort of "energy-saving mode."

What all depressions have in common is this sense of meaning-lessness to things that once brought joy. Beyond that, however, they diverge. Some people may feel constant exhaustion and need much more sleep than usual, while others may be unable to sleep or may wake up in the middle of the night with intense anxiety. Some may experience a surge in appetite and quickly pile on the pounds, while others may have no appetite at all. Some will feel restless and anx-ious, others apathetic.

It is a common misconception that depressions are caused by a deficiency in the neurotransmitters serotonin, dopamine and nor-adrenaline, but in reality things aren't quite that simple. There is no doubt that these three substances—all of which are affected by anti-depressant medication, with good results for many—play an important role in depression. Nevertheless, the image of the brain as a poorly balanced soup with only three ingredients doesn't reflect the true complexity of what depression is. It can involve a number of different regions and systems in the brain, all with the same end result: depression.

While what goes on inside the brain is both complex and differs from person to person, if we look at what triggers depression, it is surprisingly often one thing: stress. In particular, stress sustained over a long period of time—by which I mean months or years, as opposed to days or weeks—and over which we feel we have no con-trol. Stress, however, isn't the full explanation. We are also born with a high or low genetic predisposition to depression. For those who are particularly susceptible, the stress of something that isn't neces-sarily all that dramatic can be enough to trigger depression—a conflict at work, for example. For others, it may take greater levels of stress, such as the loss of a loved one. And some may never be affected at all, no matter what life throws at them. This fact is often summarized by the adage: "Genes load the gun, the environment pulls the trigger." In recent decades, gargantuan efforts have gone into trying to identify the genes that "load that gun."

When Bill Clinton announced in June 2000 that every letter in the human genome had been decoded, the president's enthusiasm knew no bounds. "We are learning the language in which God created life . . . With this profound new knowledge, humankind is on the verge of gaining immense new power to heal," the president solemnly declared. There, at the dawn of the new millennium, glimmered the prospect of eradicating the disease and suffering that had plagued us since time immemorial.

Now, some two decades on, we can say in all certainty that the sequencing of our genome truly was groundbreaking and opened up new treatment opportunities for a range of different diseases. There is, however, one exception, and that's in psychiatry— particularly depression. Researchers had hoped to find a single gene that causes depression—one gene that lies behind a biological mechanism that a pill could fix. However, no such gene exists. Nor does there exist any one gene responsible for bipolar disorder, schizophrenia or anxiety. Instead we discovered hundreds—if not thousands—of genes that all have their own small part to play in the risk of developing depression.

As hopes were dashed of finding any one weighty depression gene, a mystery crystallized. It emerged that the genes that affect our risk of developing depression tend to be common and present in many of us. If they all have a role to play—however small—in our predisposition to depression, then why are they present in so many people? Shouldn't evolution have weeded them out? After all, depression doesn't just cause misery today; for our hunter-gatherer ancestors it must have been devastating to lose the capacity for joy. Why did

Mother Nature make us so prone to depression that it now affects 280 million of us?

Relationships to viruses—not people

The insomnia was the worst. I'd go to bed early, fall asleep after an hour or so and then wake up at 2:30 with heart palpitations and this god-awful anxiety. After three weeks everything just ground to a halt. I became apathetic, stopped picking up the phone, blamed other things: I have to work, I can't. In the end, people stopped calling.

But then the tables turned and I couldn't get enough sleep. I'd be sleeping 12 hours each night but never felt rested. Every now and then I'd be overcome by this almost frantic anxiety. At one point I did briefly ponder the idea of taking my own life, to escape it. In hindsight, I'm incredibly grateful I was so apathetic that I was incapable of giving any real thought to how I might do it.

Eventually I sought help. I was prescribed medication and started doing therapy. After four months things slowly started to turn around, but it was all so gradual that I struggled to see the improvement myself. Only after six months did I start to see a light at the end of the tunnel, and today I feel fine. But I never, ever, ever want to end up there again, and I'll do everything in my power to avoid it.

This is what a 43-year-old nurse told me at an appointment to review her prescription for antidepressants. I was struck by the contrast between how well she appeared to be doing and how low she had felt before. How could things have reached a point where she even considered taking her own life? She described what had preceded her mental crash: for years she'd been living with intense stress, as both of her children had been having trouble in school and were undergoing tests for neuropsychiatric disorders. While she felt that the stress relating to her children was manageable, it was when things got hectic at work that her cup ran over, so to speak. She had been tasked with reorganizing her department's workflows—something she neither saw the point of nor felt she had any real control over. After almost a year of toil, the reorganization was finally scrapped and she was freed from her Sisyphean task. At around the same time, her children's situation improved, as they started getting better assistance from their school and child psychiatry services. And then, just when everything should have been hunky-dory, she was struck by a depression so severe that at one point she considered suicide. "It was as though the stress caught up with me right when I let my guard down," she explained.

I have lost count of the number of patients who, like this woman, have fallen into a deep depression *after* a period of intense stress. I long saw this as a sign that something had to be wrong—surely a healthy brain should rise to the challenge and get *stronger* from sustained stress, in the same way that our muscles get stronger from tough workouts? Descending into darkness once the stress had blown over had to be a sign that something was amiss.

We often view depressions, and the stress that so frequently triggers them, in terms of our relationships to others—after all, psychosocial stress often tends to be what squeezes us. But I have come to realize that from the brain's perspective we should also view them in relation to bacteria and viruses. This may sound strange and speculative, but my conclusion is based on some of the most groundbreaking medical research discoveries of recent decades. I am one of a growing number of psychiatrists and researchers who believe that our ability to develop symptoms of depression may in fact be a deep-rooted defense mechanism that historically saved us from infections. In fact, a number of

DEPRESSION

depressions—though not all—can be triggered by the immune system. This conclusion also helps to explain why so many of us are so prone to depression. But let's take a closer look at what made me start thinking in this way.

Half died in childhood

If you are someone who has a tendency to worry about getting sick, I would guess that you are most concerned about cardiovascular diseases, cancer or perhaps even Covid-19, which were all among the leading causes of death in Europe in 2020. With the exception of Covid-19, this list is extraordinary, historically speaking. In the past, it was not cancer or cardiovascular disease that tended to kill us. Throughout most of human history, roughly *half* of the population died before adulthood, mostly from infections. Read that again, because it bears repeating: *half of all humans died in childhood, mostly from infections.* The threat posed by infectious disease persisted up until just a few generations ago. As recently as the early twentieth century, the most common causes of death were pneumonia, tuberculosis and gastrointestinal infections. All of these are infectious diseases! Just four generations ago, tuberculosis claimed more human lives per capita than all forms of cancer do today.

Between 1870 and 1970, smallpox took an inconceivable 500 million lives—ten times more than World War II—with children being particularly badly affected. But getting through childhood unscathed didn't mean you were in the clear: between 1918 and 1920 a severe flu epidemic that came to be known as Spanish flu claimed the lives of at least 50 million people and was particularly fatal in 20–30-year-olds. So it wasn't World War I or even World War II that posed the greatest threat to young Westerners in the early 1900s, but smallpox and Spanish flu. If our daily papers only came out once a century, the biggest story for the twentieth century would be: "Human life expectancy doubles. Extraordinary progress in the fight against infectious disease!"

Why is this so important for understanding depression? Well, your body and brain are the result of the fact that the vast majority of humans died young, and you are the descendant of those who *didn't* die in childhood. This simple fact is extremely important since it has come to shape how our bodies and brains function. Let's take an example. Suppose two horrific infectious diseases were to strike our ancestors—we'll call them White Fever and Gray Fever. White Fever only infects children and it kills half of those who fall ill. That half of the children survive is thanks to genes they have that make them resistant. Gray Fever, on the other hand, is also fatal in half of those infected, but it only infects the over-70s. Similarly, those who survive Gray Fever do so because they have genes that make them resistant.

Let's now imagine that both White Fever and Gray Fever ravage the world's populations in a terrible pandemic. Half of all children and half of all over-70s perish. As a result, after the pandemic, all surviving children carry genes that protect them against White Fever—otherwise they would have died—and, for the very same reason, all surviving over-70s carry genes that protect them against Gray Fever. If we then jump two generations ahead, which disease will many people now have genetic protection against? The answer is White Fever. Since it affected only children, those who were at risk died before they could grow up and have children of their own. Consequently, the genes that made us more susceptible to White Fever were not passed down through the generations. By contrast, the genes that made us susceptible to Gray Fever were passed on, as those who succumbed to the disease did so late in life, by which point they had already had children who inherited those genes. By extension, this means that our bodies and brains have evolved to survive the diseases that historically killed humans when they were *young*.

NOT EVEN PRESIDENTS WERE SPARED

We have become so good at preventing early death from infectious diseases that we have completely forgotten the threat they posed until just a few generations ago. These fantastic medical advances are better illustrated by human lives than statistics. As you may know, US president Joe Biden has met with a number of personal tragedies in his life. In 1972 he lost his wife Neilia and daughter Naomi in a car crash, and in 2015 his son Beau passed away from a brain tumor. Biden's life story is something of a national trauma, and many people feel it gives him an awareness and understanding of human suffering that is unique among presidents.

Joe Biden's tragic losses may make him unique compared to other recent US presidents, but go a little further back in history and it's clear that such personal losses were more the rule than the exception. In the 1840s and 1850s, 16th president of the US Abraham Lincoln had four sons. Edward Lincoln died just shy of his fourth birthday, most likely of tuberculosis. William Lincoln died aged 11 of suspected typhoid fever. Thomas Lincoln died at 18 of tuberculosis. Only one son, Robert Lincoln, survived to adulthood. Similar tragedies befell Thomas Jefferson (the US's third president), who lost four of his six children before their second birthdays. William Harrison (9th president) had ten children and lost five. Zachary Taylor (12th president) had six children and lost three. Franklin Pierce (14th president) lost all three of his children. This continued right into the twentieth century, when Dwight Eisenhower lost one of his two sons to scarlet fever, an infectious disease.

We can count on the presidents and their families having had access to the best health care of their age. That so many of them still lost half of their children to disease is a clear reminder of something we often forget: that until just a few generations ago, most people died young. And most of them died from infections.

Different infections

Because infectious diseases have claimed so many young lives over the course of history, we have developed particularly strong defense mechanisms against them. To understand what this has to do with depression, we need to look at the types of infections that have posed a threat to us. Our species, *Homo sapiens*, emerged in Africa around 250,000 years ago. As I previously explained, throughout most of our history humans lived as hunter-gatherers, until some 10,000 years ago, when we began the gradual transition toward agriculture. Because of this, we started living in closer proximity to each other and kept animals for food. However, both of these factors made it easier for diseases to pass from animals to humans and then spread among us.

Tuberculosis, hepatitis, measles, smallpox and HIV probably all originated in animals but jumped the species barrier to humans and subsequently spread among us in our more densely populated communities. Tuberculosis, smallpox and measles are therefore probably no more than 10,000 years old, which from an evolutionary perspective makes them "new" diseases. They are the price we had to pay for living in closer communities and having the ability to feed more mouths with the food from the animals we raised. In the times of our hunter-gatherer ancestors, we probably weren't affected by these diseases, as we lived in such small groups that it would have been difficult for infections to spread.

A pandemic such as Covid-19 would have been practically impossible in hunter-gatherer times, as it requires interaction between many people from many different places. This doesn't mean that hunter-gatherers were spared from disease—far from it—only that the infections that afflicted them tended not to come from viruses and bacteria that had originated in animals. Instead, hunter-gatherers tended to suffer from infections that originated in spoiled food or wounds. Without access to antibiotics, an infected wound could have catastrophic consequences, so what did these people feel when they risked injury? Well, *stress*! The stress of the chase, of an escape, of a serious conflict. All of these things meant an increased risk of injury and the resulting risk of infection.

The American psychiatrist Charles Raison believes that, throughout most of human history, stress has been a reliable signal to the body of an increased risk of infection. The immune system expends 15–20 percent of the body's energy, making it so energy intensive that it can't be revved up all the time. Our bodies have to choose when to shift the immune system up a gear, and stress is a signal that it's time to do just that. The body, Raison believes, therefore interprets stress as a signal that there is a heightened risk of infection, as for most of our history that's precisely what stress meant. As a result, our immune system increases its activity. This mechanism didn't just apply out on the savanna; it also applies to you and me today—after all, we too are adapted for life as hunter-gatherers.

The job interview from hell

There's an interesting test that demonstrates the link between social stress and the immune system. Imagine that you are at a job interview. You enter the room to find two men and a woman in white coats sitting across from you. They look gruff and intimidating, don't say hello and ask you to get started straightaway. Hesitantly, you reel off your previous work experience and why you think it stands you in good stead for this role. You force a disarming smile to try to lighten the mood, but they just stare back at you blankly. When you pause briefly to find the right words, one of the men asks, with thinly veiled arrogance, "Do you always get this tongue-tied in interviews?"

Once you have sweated your way through the interrogation, it's time for some tests. The arrogant interviewer asks you to count back from 1,022 as quickly as possible, in intervals of 13. You start: "1,022, 1,009 . . . " after which you need a few seconds to think before saying: "996." The trio exchange mocking smiles.

This job interview from hell is part of the Trier Social Stress Test, which is used to examine how we cope with socially evaluative situations. Participants are told that they will be doing a mock job interview, which will be filmed and then evaluated by behavioral scientists. The interviewers have been instructed to appear disparaging and to respond to the interviewee with a stony face.

That the majority of participants experience discomfort, an elevated pulse and perspiration of course comes as no surprise. What makes the Trier Social Stress Test interesting is what it reveals in some participants' blood tests—namely, that their levels of interleukin-6 increase. This substance plays a key role in the immune system and stimulates fever when we have an infection. But why should levels of interleukin-6 increase during a job interview? Participants are hardly at risk of catching a virus or bacteria from those haughty interviewers— so why should the immune system mobilize against a threat to our self-esteem?

The mystery has a possible solution when we consider what we have previously discussed in this chapter. The stress that participants experience during a job interview causes the body to think we are at an increased risk of injury, since this is what stress has historically signified. As a result, the body starts to prepare. With an increased risk of injury comes an increased risk of infection, and so the immune system switches up a gear. This brings us one step closer to what all this has to do with depression.

A banquet for viruses

That our ancestors survived infections is nothing short of a miracle. Indeed, in the matchup against viruses and bacteria, we should really be doomed to lose. A virus's sole purpose is to create as many copies of itself as possible. In biological terms, a virus is only a piece of genetic code—it's even questionable whether it can be considered to be "living." As it lacks the machinery required to replicate itself, its only way to do this is to invade another organism and trick it into making these copies for it. The organism would then ideally spread the copies to others, who can in turn produce more copies and spread them even further.

From the virus's perspective, it's hard to think of a better organism to invade than a human. After all, we live in close proximity to each other, are extremely social and travel the world. What's more, we have at least 20-year intervals between our generations. Viruses, on the other hand, have only a matter of days, which means they renew roughly 10,000 times faster than we do. As a result, they are constantly mutating and appearing in new guises, making their ability to adapt much better than ours.

In other words, we are a veritable banquet for viruses and bacteria. It isn't odd that half of all children died of infections—what's strange is that we didn't *all* succumb. Before antibiotics, vaccines and modern health care, what resources did we have to combat infections? Our most obvious defense is our outstanding immune system, which remembers infections we have had before and is primed to mobilize quickly should we catch them again. Our immune system is so ingenious that it's surpassed only by the brain in complexity. And, as with the brain, our mapping of the immune system has only just begun: we are constantly discovering new functions. One personal favorite of mine is that it only takes us *seeing* someone cough to make our immune systems kick into gear.

In addition, we have a strong, reflexive dislike of spoiled food, which is the brain's way of making us avoid fare that may carry disease. Catch a whiff of sour milk or rotting fish and try not to wince. It's virtually impossible! That our immune system kick-starts at the sight of someone coughing, or that we flinch at the mere smell of spoiled food, is sometimes known as our "behavioral immune system." As the name suggests, this extended immune defense comprises our behaviors—after all, it's always better to avoid ingesting bacteria and viruses than to deal with them inside the body. And what affects behavior? Feelings! When we feel down, we withdraw, isolate ourselves and pull the duvet up over our heads. Some researchers believe that feelings of depression could be our brain's way of either helping us to avoid an infection, or conserving our energy to treat one.

In summary, the things that usually spring to mind when we think of our immune system—antibodies, B- and T-cells—are actually just *one* aspect of it. Another aspect is our behavior, through which the brain generates feelings that make us withdraw when at risk of infection. And because the body—which still believes we're out on the savanna—interprets stress as an increased risk of infection, it sees sustained, long-term stress as a looming, longstanding threat of injury and infection. In order to deal with this threat, the brain responds by creating feelings that make us withdraw and mentally stand still—in other words, depression.

Having reached this point, you might perhaps be thinking: *Yes, that theory seems reasonable enough, but how can we know that that's really how it works?* So let's take a closer look at the research.

Inflammation and feeling sick

Medical researchers long believed that the brain and the immune system were entirely separate, and that the latter could never affect the former. If a flesh wound gets infected, a group of proteins known as cytokines form, and these ensure that the immune system starts to attack the infection. But these cytokines also have another important role, which is to signal to the rest of the body that an infection is present. Until the twenty-first century, medical textbooks claimed that cytokines could send the "infection ahoy!" signal to every organ in the body, with one crucial exception: the brain. It was believed that, due to the disconnect with the immune system, these signals couldn't actually reach the brain. This was proved false by medical research in the early 2000s, when researchers discovered that cytokines can in fact enter the brain. Thus, the brain *can* pick up signals that there is inflammation somewhere in the body. Medically speaking, this discovery was a sensation, and it sparked intensified psychiatric research as researchers tried to pinpoint whether an inflammation in the body could affect how we feel and behave.

The first tests were performed on mice, who, when injected with cytokines, withdrew and behaved in a way that in humans would be interpreted as depression. These tests were followed by tests on humans, which gave the same results: after the injection, participants felt down and out of sorts.

Another lead came from patients who were receiving treatment for the liver disease hepatitis C. In the 1990s a new, very successful treatment for hepatitis C was developed, in which patients were administered with a substance typically produced by white blood cells during a viral infection. Interestingly, around one-third of these patients became depressed; despite finally receiving treatment for a potentially life-threatening illness, it was not relief that patients felt, but dejection. After the treatment, this state often passed. A similar phenomenon was observed in a number of people who were vaccinated against typhoid. For a short time they felt low in spirits, often in the hours after receiving the vaccine.

In summary, by the early 2000s a number of signs were pointing toward a link between the immune system and the brain. Contrary to what researchers had previously believed, the brain and the immune system didn't appear to be separate at all, but in fact intricately linked. Activity in the immune system appeared to have the potential to affect mental health, and an increase in immune activity seemed to be a contributing factor in depression. These suspicions were further reinforced when it was discovered that levels of proinflammatory cytokines in the spinal fluid—the fluid that surrounds the brain and spinal cord—were higher in those who were depressed.

The discovery that passed the stress test

When it comes to hot new medical research findings, there's always a risk that expectations will be overblown. When a spectacular discovery is stress-tested in major studies involving thousands of individuals, it's not uncommon for the findings to not quite live up to their earlier promise. In the early 2010s, research into the links between the immune system and depression made that precarious leap from small, promising experiments into major studies. But this time the bubble didn't burst.

When Danish researchers analyzed data from 73,000 people, they discovered that those who suffered from milder symptoms of depression, fatigue and low self-esteem often had high levels of C-reactive protein (CRP), a marker of inflammation. The higher the CRP levels, the more symptoms there were. It also emerged that the people who had high CRP levels were more likely to have been both admitted to the hospital for depression and prescribed antidepressant medication. In addition, researchers discovered that people with depression seem to have a slightly raised body temperature, i.e., a low-level fever. This may be a way of warding off infection, as fever's main function is thought to be to hamper bacteria and viruses from multiplying in the body.

The final, crucial piece of the puzzle that pointed toward a link between depression and the immune system came from genetics. I opened this chapter by saying that there is no *one* depression gene, but that many different genes have a role to play in the risk of developing depression. In fact, in one major study, 44 different genes were identified that can all be linked to depression. Many of these affect the brain and the nervous system, which isn't particularly surprising—one would expect that genes that affect the risk of depression will also affect the brain. But several of these genes also affect the immune system. They appear to have two functions: increasing the risk of depression and kicking the immune system into action.

Modern life hijacks our defense mechanisms

In order to understand why an awareness of the link between the immune system and depression is so important to feeling as mentally well as possible, we must start by dissecting two concepts that are often confused: infection and inflammation.

An *infection* is when the body is exposed to pathogens such as bacteria or a virus.

Inflammation is the body's response to basically all stimuli—everything from pressure, wounds and toxins to a bacterial or viral attack. An inflammation can be caused by an infection, but it can also be due to something else. Scratch your arm until a red mark appears: inflammation. Slip and cut your finger while slicing bread: inflammation. Your pancreas leaks digestive fluid into your abdominal cavity, putting your life at risk: inflammation.

No matter where in the body the inflammation occurs, the following happens: the cells affected by the damaged tissue, pressure, bacteria or virus send out a distress signal in the form of cytokines. This increases blood flow to the affected area so that white blood cells can reach and fight off any intruders. The increased blood flow leads to swelling, which puts pressure on the nerves and leaves the area feeling sore.

As inflammation is such a central component to many illnesses, we can easily be fooled into thinking that it's something we would be better off without. But nothing could be further from the truth. Without inflammation, we simply wouldn't survive. However, as in most of life, it's possible to have too much of a good thing. Inflammation that continues for a sustained period of time can cause problems. Heart attack, stroke, rheumatism, diabetes, Parkinson's disease and Alzheimer's disease are just a few of the health problems in which long-term inflammation has a key role to play.

In other words, long-term—chronic—inflammation lays the groundwork for a range of serious illnesses. Wherever the inflammation occurs in the body, the process is much the same: cytokines ensuring increased blood flow to the inflamed area. This raises the question of why we have such a major Achilles' heel within us—something that could potentially jeopardize multiple organs. Did evolution drop the ball? Far from it. You see, inflammation is there to protect us from the threats our ancestors faced when they were young, such as deadly bacterial and viral infections. Diseases that are caused by long-term inflammation often strike later on in life, and, as you now know, we have developed to survive that which struck down our ancestors in their youth. On the evolutionary balance, the protection that inflammation offers against bacteria and viruses outweighs the threat that it might lead to disease at an age most people historically never lived to see.

But what's even more important is that the triggers of

inflammation themselves have changed. Throughout almost all of human history, inflammations were likely primarily caused by bacterial and viral infections, wounds and injuries. Today, however, many aspects of our lifestyle can also lead to inflammation. For example, it has been proven that being seated for long periods of time leads to inflammation in muscles and fat tissue. Similarly, long-term stress (again, over months or years, as opposed to days or weeks) appears to increase the degree of inflammation throughout the entire body. Lack of sleep and environmental toxins have the same effect. Processed foods lead to inflammation in the stomach and intestines, obesity to inflammation in fat tissue, and smoking to inflammation in the lungs and respiratory tract.

The things that historically caused inflammation—bacteria, viruses and injuries—were often temporary afflictions, while today's causes—a sedentary lifestyle, obesity, stress, junk food, smoking and environmental toxins—tend to last a long time. As a result, a bodily process that was once short-lived is now running for longer than it was intended. None of this would necessarily be a problem if the body could determine the cause of the inflammation, thereby saving the immune system from unnecessary mobilization. The problem is that the body appears to lump all forms of inflammation together, mistaking lifestyle factors for attacks from viruses and bacteria.

Just as the body cannot determine whether an inflammation is caused by an infection or lifestyle factors, the same is true of the brain. Modern sources of inflammation send the same signal to the brain that viruses and bacteria do. And when this signal is left running for a long time—which tends to happen with modern sources of inflammation—the message the brain gets is: "I'm in a life-threatening situation and under constant attack!" The brain responds by regulating our mood down a notch to make us withdraw. We stand still mentally. This can continue for a sustained period of time, as modern sources of inflammation don't just fade away. The result is long-term mental stagnation—or depression, to you and me. Depression is therefore one of the many diseases that can be caused by inflammation.

Today's main sources of inflammation

Let's take a closer look at two of the main sources of inflammation of our time: long-term stress and obesity. The connection between stress and inflammation is somewhat complicated; you see, the body's main stress hormone, cortisol, mobilizes energy, but it can also dampen inflammation. When an angry dog barks at you, your cortisol levels spike to give your muscles the energy they need for you to turn on your heels and run. But once the danger has passed, the cortisol serves another purpose: to dampen inflammation in the body. In other words, the cortisol controls when the inflammation should be "turned off."

When we are exposed to long-term stress, we go around with constant high levels of cortisol in our blood, and our body eventually gets used to these levels. As a result, the body stops reacting to the cortisol, which thereby loses its ability to dampen inflammation. It's like crying wolf too many times—in the end, no one cares. So, why is this important? Well, because minor inflammations crop up all the time—small nicks in the skin, say, or minor muscle tears, or damage to blood vessels. This is completely normal. While cortisol would normally ensure that these inflammations are kept at bay, if the body stops reacting to it, then they keep on festering, increasing the degree of inflammation in the body. This is precisely what happens with long-term stress. But don't go jumping to the conclusion that all stress is dangerous: on the contrary, stress is crucial to our survival. It's just that our bodies aren't made for the stress system to be "on" all the time.

The keyword here is "recovery," and in this case that involves turning off the biological mobilization of energy that stress involves. Most of us cope well with stress, so long as we have time to recover. How much time we need is different for each individual, but a good rule of thumb is that, with a low workload, the 16 hours we have between two work shifts are often sufficient. When the workload is heavier, this calls for more recovery time, such as weekends and more time off every now and then. The point of recovery is to prioritize sleep, rest and relaxation, and to minimize other musts.

Alongside long-term stress, obesity is the other factor that creates the most inflammation in the body. Our fat tissue isn't a passive energy reserve; it sends signals to the rest of the body by releasing cytokines that activate the immune system. One might wonder why the body mobilizes the immune system against its own energy reserves, apparently viewing *itself* as a threat, and while no one has a definitive answer, one possibility could be that obesity has been virtually nonexistent in our history. As a result, the body interprets abdominal corpulence as something foreign and tries to fight off the "invading" pounds around the waistline with inflammation.

Obesity has been linked to an increased risk of depression, and while this could of course be linked to the stigma around being overweight, it could also, at least in part, be because inflammation in the fat tissues is heightening the risk of depression.

Let's summarize. You and I have evolved to live as hunter-gatherers. Our sedentary modern lifestyles and constant stress create a higher degree of inflammation than the body is built for. This is interpreted by the brain as a threat—as that is what inflammation has signified for virtually all of human history—and as a result it thinks that we are under constant attack. Hence the brain tries to make us withdraw by adjusting our feelings, which are, after all, there to guide our behavior. The brain lowers our spirits, which leads us to feel down and unwell, and in turn to withdraw. In other words, inflammation acts as a sort of thermostat for our feelings: the more inflammation we have, the worse we feel. For some of us, that thermostat appears to be particularly sensitive—determined, in part, by our genes—and this increases our susceptibility to depression.

Does this mean that everyone who has depression has an inflammatory process going on in their body? No, it doesn't. Inflammation is one of *several* major causes of depression, not the only one. It is believed that roughly one-third of all depressions are caused by inflammation. Now, you may be thinking that, if that's the case, surely anti-inflammatory medication can help to treat depression? As it happens, there's a lot of evidence to suggest just that. Medicines that block the formation of proinflammatory cytokines do have some success in treating depression, but not enough to work on their own. However, they do appear to enhance the effect of other antidepressant medications, so long as the depression is inflammation-based; otherwise their effect is negligible.

Broadened perspectives

Almost all of my patients who have depression have wondered what might have triggered it. Most suspect social factors—relationships with others, something going on at work or in school—and in this light it would naturally be difficult to understand what purpose depression could possibly serve. However, as I have described in this chapter, we should also view depression from a physiological perspective, and in terms of our relationship to bacteria and viruses. When doing so, we shouldn't assume the relatively modest threat that these pose to us now, but the fact that, for 99.9 percent of our time on earth, they cost one out of every two humans their life. As a result, symptoms of depression could be a subliminal defense mechanism that once saved us from a range of infections. In modern society, however, the triggers presented by lifestyle factors send these mechanisms into overdrive.

I have learned a few things from taking a *physiological* and not just *psychological* outlook on depression. In biological terms, depression is no stranger than pneumonia or diabetes. Neither pneumonia, diabetes nor depression have anything to do with a lack of character, so chirpily encouraging someone who is depressed to "pull themselves together" is just as absurd as saying to someone with pneumonia that they should "pull their lungs together" or that somebody with diabetes should "pull their blood sugar together." Similarly, just as one would seek medical attention for pneumonia or diabetes, one should also do so for depression.

Of course, learning more about the biology behind depressions and why they occur doesn't automatically mean that we can overcome them. But it can be a good start. Knowing how immunological processes affect my brain and how I feel has made me take well-worn lifestyle advice more seriously. Of course, you know as well as I do that we feel better if we exercise, get enough sleep and try to reduce unpredictable and long-term stress. But this advice gains a deeper significance when we realize the biological logic of why it works. When we understand that exercise, sleep, stress reduction and recovery all work to reduce inflammation, which in turn prevents the brain from receiving signals it misinterprets as an attack, we are more likely to prioritize these. However, this doesn't mean that everything that counteracts inflammation—such as certain foods—works in treating depression. Unfortunately it just isn't that simple.

This knowledge also helps us to understand why a work situation that exposes us to unpredictable stress 24/7 could lead to depression. To react to such a situation with apathy or withdrawal is not a mark of sickness; it is *healthy*. In such circumstances, the best solution is usually to change the work situation. Of course, I realize that this is easier said than done, but the point remains that an abnormal reaction to an abnormal situation is normal behavior, rather than a sickness in the brain.

The darkness will pass, even if it doesn't feel like it will right now. That's just the way we're built.

In the previous chapter, I mentioned that I have been struck by how valuable it can be to view anxiety from the brain's perspective, as this makes us less inclined to feel broken. The same is true of depression. When viewed from the brain's perspective, not only do we see that we are not "damaged goods"; we realize that depressions are transitory, as all feelings pass. When life feels unfathomably dark, it can be reassuring to remind ourselves that we are biological beings. The darkness will pass, even if it doesn't feel like it will right now. That's just the way we're built. We are not alone, either, but in the company of at least 280 million others.

To repeat, not all depressions can be explained by stress and inflammation. There may be other reasons why we might become depressed that have nothing to do with putting up a defense against bacteria and viruses but that nevertheless serve a purpose. Let's take a closer look at one of these now.

Six months of worthwhile wavering

When I was 24, I decided to make a U-turn in my life. I had almost graduated in economics from the Stockholm School of Economics, complete with having done summer internships at investment banks and consultancy firms. At the same time, however, I was wrestling with the question of whether the path this degree would lead me down was really me. This question, which had taken root on my very first day of university and grown with each passing year, was now impossible for me to ignore.

The future I had plotted for myself felt soulless. Whatever it was I wanted to accomplish—every challenge, every achievement—all boiled down to one thing: the person with the most kronor, dollars or pounds wins. In the professional world that I was on the cusp of, *everything* came down to money in the end. Was that really how I wanted to live my one life? Or should I drop everything and start over?

I can see now that this question is the very definition of a luxury problem. To be weighing up whether to turn down such a silver platter of opportunity while still wet behind the ears isn't exactly much of a crisis in life. I can also see that the decision should have been an easy one; the only thing at stake was a change of degree course, and I was still so young. But in my unhealthily competitive 24-year-old eyes, I might as well have been halfway to retirement. At the time it felt like a big deal to change track so "late" in life, and the fact that it would mean losing four years was not a decision I took lightly.

For one whole winter and spring I withdrew. Brooding and sleepless, I churned the question around and around in my head. I mulled it over, made a decision and then changed my mind. Changed it back, then back again. I felt down and generally unmotivated, and I had trouble concentrating on anything but my ruminations, even though I kept them all to myself. One year later I stepped into the great auditorium at the Karolinska Institutet to start studying medicine. In retrospect I can see that this was one of the most important decisions I have ever made, and I have often wondered whether my period of low spirits was what allowed me to make the decision I eventually came to.

As a psychiatrist, I have observed that many of my patients who are experiencing mental health problems are also grappling with big, important decisions. They rarely say it in so many words, but if I ask the question, it often hits the mark. One woman told me that she was considering leaving her partner. A man was contemplating quitting a job that he had stayed in for far too long and making a career change. Another patient had been applying to drama school for years and, after a number of unsuccessful attempts, was now deciding whether to give up on their acting dreams for good. Every time I meet a patient like this, I recognize my dithering 24-year-old self. They churn the question around and around in their heads. Mull it over, make a decision and then change their mind. Change it back, then back again. All the while feeling down.

Having followed them for several years, I have been struck by how things work out for the majority of them in the end, just as they did for me. Like me, many of them feel that, however unpleasant it was, this period of pondering and vacillation was essential for them to be able to make that big decision—as though everything had to be brought to an emotional head. After all, life is one long string of decisions, and in most of these our brain's autopilot works very well indeed. However, some decisions can't be taken lightly. Could it be that our brains work differently when faced with life-changing decisions? Might symptoms of depression be a way of shielding ourselves from day-to-day distractions so that we can devote all our energy to considering an important question?

Naturally, my personal experience is far from enough here, so let's turn to the research once again. Interestingly, there are studies that explore how the way we feel affects our mental faculties. In one such study, children were shown video clips and played music that made them feel either cheerful or sad. Afterward, they were made to do a psychological test, which involved quickly finding patterns in a figure and required attention to detail. Personally, I would have expected the cheerful children to perform better, but the opposite proved true: the cheerful children actually performed *worse* than the sad ones. One possible interpretation is that we stop looking for flaws when we feel good—why go looking for problems when there are none? When we feel good, we have a tendency to process over-arching information at the expense of the fine print. Interestingly, we appear to be slightly more easily deceived when we feel good—perhaps because we don't analyze the details with such a critical eye. When we are down, however, we do the opposite—we process the information with a fine-tooth comb, seeking out flaws.

Now, of course, being in a cheerful or dejected state of mind induced by music is not the same thing as being happy or depressed, but the studies still reveal something interesting: the way we feel appears to go hand in hand with our mental faculties. And the facul-ties we need at certain times vary. At times we may need critical, meticulous problem-solving abilities—the ability to stop and think, zoom in on threats and challenges and ponder questions again and again and again until they are resolved. At this point the brain makes us feel down because being low goes hand in hand with the cognitive capacities we need. At other times, it's better to be able to see the overarching picture and be more proactive and open to risk; in these scenarios the brain makes us feel good because a positive (or "high") mood enables us to adopt those characteristics.

That such a withdrawal could be our brain's strategy when ana-lyzing a life-changing problem is known as the "analytical rumination hypothesis." I will never know if this is what I experienced that winter and spring some 20 years ago. My point is not that a listless melan-choly is always good for us—on the contrary, it can often be destructive or even paralyze us in the face of a decision. Rather, it's that the type of mental faculties that go hand in hand with depression can be good to have in our mental repertoire, in the same way that it has been beneficial to us to be able to take to our heels when we need to.

Does this sound far-fetched? If so, consider whether at any point in your life you have felt down and perhaps withdrawn, and if that time ultimately took you somewhere worthwhile. Perhaps you made your mind up about a question that had long been nagging you. Perhaps you wouldn't undo that experience because you learned something from it. Perhaps you have had one of these experiences, perhaps not. That something can be useful doesn't mean it always is.

So, there can be completely healthy reasons why the brain might lower your spirits to the extent that it gives you depression, which hasn't got the slightest thing to do with stress or an age-old defense against bacteria and viruses. That being said, most things about the brain are complex, and that's particularly true when it comes to depression. Often it can be difficult to give a definitive answer as to why someone might be depressed. The reality isn't black or white, but endless shades of gray. We can't say that *all* depressions serve a purpose or are caused by either inflammation or our musings on life-changing decisions. Still, on that gray scale that begins with a very manageable psychosocial stress and ends in biological defense mechanisms that are difficult to rein in, we often underestimate the importance of biology. Even if most depressions contain an element of dysfunctional brooding that serves no purpose, they can also sometimes bring an element of withdrawal that gives us the space to make a life-changing decision.

If we believe that the presence of anxiety and depression automatically means that the brain is broken or sick, we have forgotten that the brain's primary purpose is survival and not well-being. Of course, this doesn't change the fact that depressions and anxiety can incapacitate, break down and kill people. In the following chapters, we will take a closer look at a few crucial keys to treating, and above all preventing depression and anxiety from the brain's perspective. We will start with something that you perhaps associate with boredom, but which historically has been an almost certain death sentence: loneliness.

CHAPTER 5

LONELINESS

The soul shudders before the void, and seeks contact at all costs.

HJALMAR SÖDERBERG, *DOCTOR GLAS*

IMAGINE A MEDICAL condition that affects over one-third of us, and which for one in twelve is so acute that it's as dangerous as smoking one pack of cigarettes per day. This condition exists. It's called loneliness. One of the most unexpected medical research discoveries of recent decades is that friends and relatives not only make our lives fuller—they also make them longer and healthier. The rather bleak flipside is that their absence puts our health at risk. In this chapter we'll take a closer look at how loneliness affects us, and why its impact on both brain and body is as powerful as it is—and, of course, what we can do about it.

But before we go any further, what is loneliness, exactly? In an unusually dry definition—even by medical standards—it is described as "a concerning disparity between the desired level of social interaction and the level experienced." This definition stresses an important point: loneliness is the difference between how much social interaction we have and how much we would like to have. As social needs differ from person to person, it isn't possible to quantify loneliness in the number of Facebook friends, invitations to dinner, Christmas cards or phone calls we get. Personally, I'm quite happy in my own company and don't need that many people around me to feel good, while a number of my friends all but panic if they have to spend a few hours on their own. Loneliness is therefore subjective and it *isn't* the same thing as being alone. We can feel a powerful sense of closeness to others even when we are alone, and we can feel isolated even with many people around us. In short: if you feel lonely, you are lonely. If you don't, you aren't—whatever the state of your social life.

If you are concerned about the health impact of short bouts of loneliness, let me reassure you: it takes long periods of time—for example, quite a few months or years—for the risk of illness to rise. Feeling lonely for short periods of time is not only not dangerous, it's pretty much impossible to avoid. Loneliness is a natural facet of our biology and something that almost all of us experience from time to time. Expecting never to experience loneliness is just as unrealistic as expecting never to experience anxiety.

Loneliness and depression

It can come as no surprise that loneliness increases the risk of depression, but most people don't realize how closely linked depression and loneliness really are. According to one study, people with depression are ten times more likely to feel lonely than the population at large. After just a few months working as a psychiatrist, I was struck by how many of my patients—whether they were in their twenties, middle-aged or older—felt lonely and isolated. Some had been lonely for a while, but for the majority their loneliness appeared to coincide with their depression. This made me wonder whether depressions are a byproduct of loneliness or the cause of us withdrawing and isolating ourselves. What comes first: depression or loneliness?

A group of researchers in Australia studied over 5,000 people with an average age of 50. The participants were asked a range of questions about how they were feeling and how many social groups they were involved in. The groups could be nonprofit, political or religious associations, or just a group of people practicing a shared hobby. These ranged from book clubs, choirs, cooking groups, sewing circles and sports clubs to parish groups, kennel clubs, bridge clubs and the office softball team.

Two years later, the same people were asked to respond to the questions once again. As it happened, some of the participants who had shown signs of depression in the first survey showed no such signs in the second. Of those whose problems had eased, a large percentage had been involved in one or more social groups in the two years that had passed between the surveys. Tackling loneliness by seeking out and getting involved in social groups was thereby linked to improved prospects of recovery. This is a sign that loneliness often—though of course not always—comes first and depression follows. If the loneliness is disrupted, there is a greater chance that the depression will pass.

What's interesting about this study is not only that the impact of social groups was significant, but that it increased in line with the number of groups participants were involved in. Those who were involved in one social group had a 24 percent lower risk of depression, while for those who were involved in three groups that same risk was reduced by 63 percent. With figures like that, one could easily infer that isolation and loneliness could be substantial contributing factors to the depressions we see today. Indeed, there is much to suggest that this is the case. An ambitious study that followed some 4,200 participants over the course of 12 years revealed that almost 20 percent of all depressions in people aged 50 and over stemmed from loneliness. The researchers suggested that one in five of those who had depression had developed it as a result of loneliness.

A surprising finding

The brain isn't the only thing that is impacted by loneliness; the rest of the body is, too. One group of researchers decided to find out why certain people who suffer from heart disease survive while others don't. They followed over 13,000 people who had suffered a heart attack or who suffered from arrhythmia, heart failure or heart valve disease. The participants had to disclose whether they smoked or drank, which diseases they had in the family and their general state of health. They were also asked a few unexpected questions relating to whether they often felt lonely and whether they had someone to talk to if they needed to.

When the researchers followed up a few years later, it emerged that people with heart disease who smoked and drank a lot ran an increased risk of death—but that those who felt lonely did, too. No matter what type of heart disease they had, the risk of death was almost twice as high in people who felt lonely. Could this be caused by the fact that lonely people lead unhealthier lives? After all, lonely people tend not to have someone around to tell them to get out and exercise, put out that cigarette or cut down on the junk food. To explore this, the researchers cleared exercise, smoking and food from their calculations. Even so, loneliness was still a contributing factor to an early death. It appeared to be dangerous *in itself*.

The same bleak pattern emerged in a survey of almost 3,000 women with breast cancer. Those who were lonely and socially isolated passed away from their cancer in greater numbers. When data from 148 studies involving a combined total of over 300,000 participants were compiled, the presence of friends and social support networks was so strongly linked to a reduced risk of death following a stroke or heart attack that it was on a par with such major and well-known preventive factors as quitting smoking and getting regular exercise. In other words, when it comes to the Western world's most common and fourth most common causes of death (cardiovascular disease and strokes respectively), loneliness sparked an increased risk of death so great that it was comparable to smoking. Given the discoveries I have just mentioned, a number of researchers have drawn the conclusion that loneliness is as dangerous as smoking 15 cigarettes per day. The first time I read this I was shocked. How could loneliness be harmful to the body?

Loneliness—fight or flight

As we know, the brain directs the body's organs with the help of many nerves. The majority of this happens beyond our control—you don't have to give any thought to how your brain, intestines or liver do their jobs. This involuntary part of the nervous system, our autonomic nervous system, consists of two parts: the *sympathetic* and *parasympathetic* nervous systems. The sympathetic nervous system is associated with our fight-or-flight response and is activated if we get scared, angry or wound up. This makes our pulse and blood pressure rise and sends blood to our muscles in readiness to take action—i.e., to go on the offensive or take to the hills.

In contrast to the sympathetic system we have the parasympathetic system, which is associated with digestion and calm. This part of the nervous system is activated when we exhale slowly, as briefly touched upon in the chapter on anxiety. The parasympathetic nervous system lowers our pulse and sends blood to the stomach and intestines in order to digest food. Both parts of the autonomic nervous system are active within you right now, and which one is dominant is continuously changing. When you run for the bus or feel nervous ahead of an important presentation, the sympathetic takes command. Once the presentation is over and you sit down for lunch, the parasympathetic is dominant.

It wouldn't be such a stretch to assume that loneliness activates the parasympathetic nervous system. After all, a lonely person has time to unwind and no one to fight or flee from. But, strange as it may seem, the opposite is in fact true. Loneliness activates the sympathetic nervous system and is linked to our fight-or-flight response rather than calm or digestion.

That long-term loneliness prepares the body to fight or flee is only the first in a long line of seemingly paradoxical discoveries around loneliness. These include the discovery that we perceive our surroundings and other people as more threatening when we are lonely. We become more sensitive to other people's facial expressions and interpret these differently. Neutral expressions appear slightly threatening, while slightly unsympathetic faces feel outright hostile. The brain is hypersensitive to signs that others might view us negatively, and this means that we perceive the people around us as competitive and unhelpful. Acquaintances start to feel like strangers. In short, when we're lonely, the world becomes less welcoming and more menacing.

Strength in numbers

It is impossible to say for certain why we work like this, but, as is so often the case, we find a likely explanation by casting our gaze back in time. For 99.9 percent of our time on earth, humans have depended on each other for survival. The few who survived all of the hazards and disasters that nature threw at them—and in doing so became our ancestors—did it together. That you are reading this book is an upshot of the fact that they stuck together and protected each other. Togetherness was tantamount to survival, and this meant that those who were equipped with a strong urge to create and nurture social ties had better odds of making it through. As descendants of these survivors, you and I have inherited a deeply rooted instinct to create and nurture these social ties. In other words, the brain rewards togetherness with well-being, but for purely selfish reasons:

it increased our chances of survival. Conversely, the discomfort that loneliness causes is the brain's way of telling us that we need to address our social needs. When we are lonely, we are in a state that the brain interprets as an increased risk of death—as that's precisely what loneliness has meant to us for almost all of human history.

This perspective makes it easier to understand why loneliness is linked to the fight-or-flight response rather than digestion and rest. As the brain sees it, if we are lonely, we have no one to help us, and therefore we need to be on the lookout for dangers. We adopt a constant state of alertness, which results in low-level, long term stress in the body. The sympathetic nervous system is dominant. Long-term stress has in turn been linked to elevated blood pressure and an increased degree of inflammation. This is both a possible and plausible explanation as to why loneliness brings with it a worse prognosis in cardiovascular diseases and more.

So, loneliness means that the brain amps up its alertness and that our surroundings appear more threatening than they are. This might just have saved our lives historically, but for you and me it does more harm than good. Our social lives are hardly likely to improve if we view others as hostile; instead, we risk appearing arrogant and unfriendly. Similarly, second-guessing others' intentions can by extension make us pull away: "They probably don't really want me to come to the party, I might as well not go." This eventually becomes a vicious cycle in which we pull away more and more and see the world around us in an ever more negative light: "They definitely don't want me to come. They only invited me because they felt bad or want something from me. No way am I going."

As if that wasn't enough, it has also been proven that sleep becomes more fragmented when we're lonely for a long time. We don't sleep any less, but our sleep becomes shallower and we wake up more often. Of course, it sounds dubious that someone who is sleeping alone should be punished with shorter periods of deep sleep;

why, if they have no one tossing and turning next to them, should they wake up more often? Here, too, history offers us a likely explanation. If someone was sleeping alone, they would have no one to warn them about dangers, so it was important that they slept lightly and stirred at the slightest noise.

Worse than accidents

That the brain perceives loneliness as a danger was clearly proven when one group of study participants was asked to complete a rigged personality test. Regardless of how they responded, some participants were told that their personality traits meant that they ran a heightened risk of ending up lonely in life. Others were told that their personality traits were associated with an increased risk of accidents. And others were told that their personality traits meant that they had good prospects for a rich social life with many friends, and no added risk of accidents.

Immediately after the test results were given, participants took part in a number of cognitive tests that assessed their IQ, concentration and memory. Those who were told that they ran a risk of loneliness performed worse in the tests than those who were told that they would lead an abundantly social, accident-free life. Of course, this is unsurprising. If we hear that we risk being lonely, our brains immediately start to analyze what we could do to avoid exclusion. *How can I prevent myself from being ousted from the group?* As a result, our concentration wavers and we can be expected to perform worse on cognitive tests. The same was true of those who were told that they risked being involved in accidents; they too performed worse on the tests. This is also unsurprising: if you discover that you run a risk of being in an accident, your brain will immediately start to analyze what it could do to avoid that. Your concentration wavers, which is reflected in poorer test results.

What's interesting is that those who were told that their

personality traits increased their risk of loneliness performed worse on the tests than those who were told that they had a greater risk of being involved in accidents. From the brain's perspective, future loneliness appears to pose a greater threat than future accidents. Consequently, loneliness is a condition that the brain does all it can to avoid, taking top priority even over accidents. Consider how attentive we are to social signals that suggest we might be excluded. *Why hasn't she called? Why haven't I been invited to the wedding? Why have they posted a picture of a picnic when they never asked if I wanted to come along?* The difficulty we experience in banishing these thoughts from our minds stems from the fact that, throughout almost all of human history, signals relating to exclusion were a sign that something was very seriously wrong and could even cost us our lives. They required immediate action.

In practice, excluding someone—be that not inviting them to a party, or ghosting them—is essentially the same thing as sending them a signal that they no longer belong to the group. This is interpreted by the brain as an urgent issue—perhaps even a threat to survival—and drives up activity in the sympathetic nervous system. On the other hand, including someone—sending an invitation, calling or messaging them—sends a signal that they belong. Deep in the recipient's psyche, age-old mechanisms will interpret this as someone being there to help them if anything should happen. The brain no longer sees a heightened risk of danger and the sympathetic nervous system can switch down a gear.

ISOLATION VS. STARVATION

Researchers at the Massachusetts Institute of Technology had volunteers spend ten hours stuck in total isolation in window-less rooms with no access to mobile phones. Afterward, they performed a magnetic resonance imaging (MRI) scan on them to study their brains. To ensure that the participants didn't see a single soul during the experiment, they were instructed on how to position themselves in the MRI scanner on their own. Once in place, they were shown images of people spending time together. When this happened, a region deep within the brain known as the "substantia nigra" was activated. The more participants stated that they longed to see people, and the richer the social life they had, the greater the activation.

The participants were then asked to fast for ten hours and do another MRI scan, and this time they were shown images of food. Interestingly enough, the pattern of activity in the substantia nigra was similar to that observed when they were shown images of people together. However, the pattern of activity differed in other parts of the brain, such as the reward system, based on whether it was food or company that the participants were craving.

The researchers behind the study believe that the substantia nigra sends out a *general* signal of longing—be that for food, company or something else. The activity in other brain areas varies based on what it is we want. That the brain employs similar neuronal machinery for both hunger and a desire for social interaction suggests that, from the brain's perspective, the instinct to create and nurture social relationships is just as fundamental to us as eating.

Sound familiar?

Why have I devoted so much of this chapter to describing why the brain reacts the way it does to loneliness? Well, because this knowledge is important to combat it. If you feel lonely, it's worth thinking about whether the psychological ramifications you have just read about match your own experience. Perhaps you see the world as being more threatening and hostile than it really is, or perhaps you see yourself in a much worse light than you should. If you do, it's a sign that your brain is reacting exactly the way it's supposed to.

Ask yourself if that interaction with another person—the one you felt went so badly—really was all that bad. When you reacted negatively to what a colleague, school friend or random passerby said, might it be that you were attaching too much weight to the negative? Of course, the answer here might well be no, but when we are lonely it can be a good idea to not always listen to our thoughts—in the same way that it's a good idea not to listen to our thoughts when we have anxiety. Learning more about how loneliness affects us in order to combat it is also a piece of advice that the science backs up. When American researchers compiled the results from multiple studies that compared different approaches to beating loneliness—everything from social competence training to support groups—it emerged that the most effective method was to learn, systematically and in therapy, how loneliness affects our thought patterns and our perceptions of ourselves.

Naturally, recognizing these mechanisms is equally important in helping others to overcome loneliness. That our fellow beings occasionally come across as prickly and unsympathetic isn't necessarily a sign that they dislike you or don't want any help; it could just as easily be a symptom of loneliness.

The value of small gestures

Of course, in practice it's far from easy to try to view ourselves and our thoughts from a bird's-eye perspective and see how loneliness affects us. So what else can we do? In the winter of 2021, when the whole world was beset by isolation and lockdowns, one study offered up an important piece of the puzzle. A group of researchers studied 240 people aged between 27 and 101, the majority of whom lived alone and were considered to be at-risk for experiencing long-term loneliness. Participants were asked a number of questions about the loneliness and isolation they were experiencing, and based on their responses they were given a "loneliness score." After that, the participants were called a few times each week to talk about, well, anything. The phone calls generally lasted no more than ten minutes.

After four weeks of phone calls the participants were asked the same questions again and a new loneliness score was calculated. It turned out to be 20 percent lower than before. Reductions in anxiety and symptoms of depression were also observed. How could the occasional short phone call have such a markedly positive effect? Had the participants been speaking to psychologists with decades of training in how to deliver perfectly balanced, razor-sharp guidance in line with the latest research? Not in the slightest. The voices on the other end of the line were a group of young people aged between 17 and 23 who had received just one hour of training in empathic conversations. This training can be summarized in a few lines: listen to who you are talking to; be interested in what they have to say; let them choose the topic of conversation.

The study lasted just four weeks, but let's imagine it ran for years. In that amount of time, it's actually possible that those short phone calls would have resulted in participants feeling less lonely, and consequently gaining a health benefit equivalent to quitting smoking.

How much social interaction is enough?

Let's circle back to the study that showed that the more social groups participants were involved in, the greater the reduction in their risk of depression. This raises a question: is more socializing always better, or can we have too much of a good thing? What is "enough" when it comes to friends? Although research into loneliness is still an emerging field, and there are also many disparities from person to person, it appears to be much more important that we feel a strong sense of belonging to a few people than to be constantly booked up with social engagements. The most important protection appears to be found in having a limited number of close friends around whom you can feel relaxed.

In one of the most celebrated psychological studies of all time, it was shown that a few close relationships are more important than many superficial ones. The study started in the late 1930s, when researchers at Harvard University set out to learn what made for a happy life. Such an ambitious point of inquiry calls for an equally ambitious study, and on that front it certainly didn't disappoint. The researchers recruited 500 students and their non-student peers from poorer parts of greater Boston, and they were all asked to take part in regular interviews and undergo health checks. As the years passed and participants started their own families, their partners and children were also interviewed as part of the study.

The study was intended to last 15 years, but eight decades on it's still going strong. Some participants have been followed from the age of 20 to over 90. Some saw fantastic success; one of them—John F. Kennedy—even became president of the US. When the interview responses, tests and other data were compiled, it became clear that what mattered most to the vast majority of participants was neither money nor status, fame or even power, but good relationships with their family, friends and colleagues. Psychiatrist George Vaillant, who led the study for over 30 years, summarizes the results better than any figures or tables can: "When the study began, nobody cared about empathy or attachment. But the key to healthy aging is relationships, relationships, relationships."

The Harvard study opened the door for a number of fascinating discoveries, and I very much recommend taking a look at it if you are interested in human well-being. One interesting finding is that it didn't matter so much if relationships had their ups and downs over the course of a life (i.e., if there were periods when those relationships were less fulfilling); what mattered was the knowledge that someone would be there if anything should happen. Another finding was that the experience of loneliness often changed over the course of a lifetime. Some people felt extreme loneliness as 25-year-olds but not later on in life. According to psychiatrist Robert Waldinger, the current director of the study, personality is not "set like plaster" by 30; things change.

The physical dimension of our social needs

During the Covid-19 pandemic, our digital resources became an indispensable lifeline to the rest of the world. As more and more work meetings, yoga classes, after-work drinks and doctors' appointments moved online, we dedicated more time to the virtual world than the real. It didn't take long before studies from around the world started to show that many people were feeling stressed and lonely. Of course, it's not surprising that we would experience intense stress when being bombarded with information about a pandemic, given the threat that other contagious diseases have posed to us. But what led to that increased sense of loneliness, when our connected societies give us every opportunity to see each other digitally? Why couldn't our screens satisfy our social needs? In medical research it often isn't possible to give a 100 percent clear-cut answer, but we do get a clue from our skin. It contains receptors that only react to light touch—not to pain, temperature or a firm squeeze, but to light touch alone.

Why has evolution gone to the trouble of equipping us with hardware that registers only light touch? One clue comes from the fact that these receptors react if the skin is touched at a speed of up to about an inch per second, which just so happens to be the same speed as a caress. Another clue is to be found if we follow their signal pathways, which run from the skin to the back of the pituitary gland at the base of the brain. The pituitary gland reacts by releasing a group of substances that go by the umbrella term "endorphins." These relieve pain and create a strong sense of well-being.

A third clue comes from our cousins in the animal kingdom, since these receptors also happen to be found in chimpanzees and gorillas. These animals devote up to 20 percent of their waking hours to activating these receptors by tweaking each other's fur. This behavior is called "grooming." The animals' grooming behavior cannot be motivated by a need to keep the fur clean, as this likely wouldn't take up one-fifth of their waking hours. Interestingly, stroking the fur also serves a social purpose, by which both the ape doing the grooming and the one being groomed experience a release of endorphins that creates a bond between them. As the apes tend to each other's fur across their entire group, it gives the opportunity for group bonding.

Gorillas and chimpanzees normally live in groups of 20–30 individuals and grooming therefore works well to nurture and strengthen social bonds within the troop. But since we can only groom one on one, there's a limit to the size of group that it can effectively bond. As we saw at the beginning of this book, historically humans lived in groups of up to 150 people, which is too many to be bonded by grooming. If you had to pat that many people every day, you wouldn't have time for anything else.

Group grooming

British anthropologist Robin Dunbar decided to see whether there are behaviors that make the brain release endorphins in more than just two individuals (i.e., the one grooming and the one being groomed), thereby enabling group grooming. He suspected that laughter could have this effect, and to test his hypothesis he had a group of strangers go to the movie theater and watch a comedy together. As a point of comparison, he had another group of strangers watch a long, boring documentary instead. Endorphins, however, are difficult to measure, as they don't pass through the brain's blood vessels. Even if we measure endorphin levels in the blood, this gives us no idea what the levels actually are in the brain. So Dunbar turned endorphins' effect as painkillers to his advantage. He made participants hold their hands in a sink of ice-cold water and measured how long they could withstand the cold.

Dunbar reasoned that, since an endorphin spike should increase participants' pain threshold, it would allow them to keep their hands in the ice water longer. And, sure enough, those who had watched a comedy together kept their hands in the cold water longer! What's even more interesting is that they experienced a budding sense of closeness to each other. They entered the theater as strangers and left with an inkling of togetherness. In the group that had watched the boring documentary, the pain threshold remained unchanged and there was no sense of community.

But was it really the endorphins that made the comedy-goers feel that sense of community? To find out, Dunbar and a group of Finnish researchers conducted another study using so-called PET technology. PET is short for "positron emission tomography," a method that involves being injected with a radioactive substance that binds to other substances—including endorphins. After being injected with the substance, participants were asked to laugh—and, indeed, they released endorphins! So yes, laughing together really does appear to have the same function as apes picking each other's fur—with the important distinction that laughter can strengthen the bond between more than just two individuals. This could explain why we laugh 30 times more often together. Yes, there really is research into that.

Dunbar decided to see whether other, less positive feelings can function in the same way, so he had a group of strangers watch a more emotionally fraught film starring the actor Tom Hardy. In the film, Hardy plays a homeless, extremely troubled addict who takes his own life. It turned out to have the same effect as the comedy: tolerance to pain increased and the group experienced a budding sense of belonging. So, if you feel uplifted when leaving the theater and perhaps spontaneously chat with other spectators about how good the film was, it's probably because you have had an endorphin rush that has created a sense of togetherness.

But experiencing a tragic or comic story with others is only the beginning. Dance with others and the body releases endorphins. The same applies to singing and exercise, particularly if you do them in groups. The sense of togetherness that you experience while singing along at a concert, watching a moving drama on stage, laughing away at a comedy at the movie theater or even doing a group exercise class appears to be caused by the brain releasing endorphins, which creates a sense of unity with the people around you. Dunbar believes that behaviors such as laughing, dancing and sharing funny or poignant stories have evolved as more effective forms of grooming. This has made it possible for us to stick together in larger groups than our cousins in the animal kingdom. So, in summary, culture really does appear to be vital!

What all of these activities have in common is the fact that we have to do them *together*—a number of people have to experience the same feelings at the same time. Why is this so important to recognize in an age that has seen more and more group activities move online? Well, the brain's use of endorphins—in itself stimulated by physical touch—seems to be the key player in the biochemistry around friendship and closeness. This gives a strong indication that there is a purely physical dimension to our unshakable social needs. The fact that during the pandemic we were deprived of this physical dimension gives us a possible explanation as to why so many people felt lonely. We need to see each other in real life, share touch and be in physical proximity to each other, for the simple reason that our strong social needs evolved from just that during millions of years of evolution. It seems that we can transfer some of this social support to the screen, but not all of it.

Dunbar believes that, although social media and digital communications can help us to maintain relationships that might otherwise have drifted apart, it's hard to form new close and meaningful relationships through the screen. When we meet face to face, it also signals—particularly in our digital age—that we want to make the effort. As there are only 24 hours in a day, the more time we spend online, the less we have to meet up in real life. If someone can invent virtual touch, they will be deserving of a Nobel Peace Prize, Dunbar suggests. This would facilitate a sense of belonging between millions, possibly even billions, of people. But pending the invention of virtual touch, it would be wise for us to remember that there is a purely physical dimension to our social needs.

Our increasingly digital lifestyles also have an impact on our state of mind that has nothing to do with a lack of physical proximity but is nevertheless a facet of loneliness. Let's take a closer look at that now.

WHEN ARE WE AT OUR MOST LONELY?

Studies from a number of different countries show that between 20 and 30 percent of the population often feel lonely and isolated. How this sense of loneliness fluctuates over the course of a lifetime obviously varies from person to person, but despite this individual variation, there are a few patterns that offer some food for thought. Among young people aged between 16 and 24 this figure is between 30 and 40 percent. In the

35–45-year-old age range roughly one-third of people feel lonely, while those who are over 45 often feel less lonely. This may be due to the fact that, with age, we become more selective in our socializing and prioritize the people who mean the most to us. The age group that feels the least lonely is those in their sixties. However, after 85, sadly, loneliness rises again, presumably because many lose partners as well as friends.

Hollowed needs

If you are an adult, you spend on average between three and four hours per day on your phone. If you are a teenager, that figure is between five and six hours—roughly half of your waking hours outside of school. Our new digital age has brought with it the most rapid behavioral change in human history, and how it affects the way we feel remains a huge question mark. Still, we need go no further than the figures you just read to see what is perhaps its most significant cost. Given that there are only 24 hours in a day, more hours spent in front of a screen means less of something else: less time to meet up in real life, less time for exercise and less time for sleep. As a result, hardly anyone can be surprised that, since the turn of the millennium, the average number of steps walked by 14-year-olds has dropped by 30 percent in boys and 24 percent in girls, or that the number of teenagers seeking help for insomnia and being prescribed sleeping pills has increased by almost 1,000 percent in the same period.

When it comes to how we feel, the main issue isn't what we do with our phones, but what *gets cut* in favor of screen time. Our means of nurturing mental health—sleep, exercise and socializing in real life—are gradually being hollowed out by our increasingly digital lifestyles. But can a lot of time in front of the screen be dangerous *in itself*? As we will see a little further on, it isn't possible to say for sure whether we feel worse today than we did 20 or 30 years ago. There is, however, one exception, and that is in teenagers, particularly girls. This group has seen a clear increase in mental health problems. One of many examples is a study in which 62 percent of the girls surveyed stated that they had multiple chronic symptoms of stress, such as anxiety, stomachache and sleep disorders. This is more than twice what the figure was in the 1980s. In boys that figure was 35 percent, twice what it was in the 1980s. The same grim pattern can be observed in a large number of countries.

Why this dramatic rise in mental health problems has affected girls in particular is difficult to say for sure, but I will take the liberty of speculating. Teenagers devote around half of their waking hours after school to their phones. Girls largely spend this time on social media, while boys spend it gaming. To see how this might contribute to a more rapid increase in mental health problems in girls, let's take a look at this from the brain's perspective.

The urge to compare ourselves to others

If you place your finger an inch or so behind your earlobe and from that point drill straight into the brain, you will reach what in medical circles are termed the "raphe nuclei," which consist of roughly 150,000 brain cells. Despite only containing some 0.0002 percent of the brain's cells, the raphe nuclei are crucial to how we function and feel. This is where the majority of one of the brain's most fascinating substances is made—by which I mean serotonin.

In many countries, more than one in ten adults are currently being treated with antidepressants, mostly selective serotonin reuptake inhibitors (SSRIs), which increase serotonin levels. How can it be that we have developed this seemingly inexhaustible need to boost our serotonin? What universal, virtually unlimited human need do these medicines fulfill? To try to understand this, let's return to the brain.

After the serotonin is produced in the raphe nuclei, it is transported via at least 20 different signal pathways to basically the entire brain. In doing so, it affects a number of different mental characteristics, which means that its effects are extremely complex. But what is probably its most important task can actually be described very simply: serotonin regulates the extent to which we withdraw. And that isn't only true of humans.

Serotonin can be traced back at least a billion years in history and it affects withdrawal in many other species. If the three-spined stickleback and zebrafish are exposed to serotonin-boosting medication at levels that have been recorded outside sewage treatment works, they become less cautious and run a greater risk of being eaten by predators. When the finely tuned equilibrium that regulates withdrawal, honed over millions of years, is upset, it becomes a matter of life and death. For fish this threat often comes from another species, but in other animals it can also come from members of the same species. Lobsters, for example, are known to fly at each other in violent skirmishes. Such conflicts are usually defused before they come to blows by the more dominant lobster forcing its adversary to fold. But if a lobster gets a dose of serotonin-boosting medication, it becomes more domineering and less likely to back down. In short, the lobster's concept of its position in the hierarchy changes if its serotonin levels change. The same is true in chimpanzees. When an alpha male or female is ousted, a power vacuum appears. If a randomly chosen chimpanzee is then given serotonin-boosting medication, it will tend to take the lead and become the new alpha male or female.

In humans, too, serotonin seems to affect how we perceive our place in the hierarchy (and the reverse is probably also true: our perceived place in the hierarchy affects serotonin). For example, one study of university students at an American student dorm revealed that students who had been there for a long time and had leadership roles had higher serotonin levels than new members. But what does all this have to do with mental health in teens? Well, serotonin doesn't only affect our position in the hierarchy; it also affects our emotional lives. The most commonly used medications for treating depression affect our serotonin levels, and these medicines help many people to feel better. This means that there is a very close biological link between our perceived position in the hierarchy and how we feel. If we are pushed down in the hierarchy, we are more inclined to feel low. And never have there been so many reasons to feel pushed down as today, with social media constantly forcing us to compare ourselves to others' perfect lives. In a nutshell: from a "serotonin perspective" there have never been so many reasons to feel down as now.

A VALUABLE DISCOVERY

The discovery of serotonin is not just an exciting piece of science; it also resulted in some of the most widely sold medications of all time.

In the mid-1930s, Italian chemist Vittorio Erspamer was investigating the coordination of the digestive system's motor function when he discovered a substance that made the intestines contract. At first he thought it was adrenaline, but that wasn't the case. Nor did it match up with a number of other known substances. Erspamer realized that he had discovered a previously unknown substance, which he named "enteramine" after "enter-", which in medical terminology signifies the intestines.

One decade on, when the American doctor Irvine Page was working to map the physiological mechanisms that cause high blood pressure, he discovered a substance in the blood that had the same vasoconstrictive effect. It turned out to be identical to enteramine. As the liquid that our blood cells are found in is called "serum," enteramine was given a new name: serotonin. Page was in the midst of charting the role serotonin plays in high blood pressure when he was contacted by 25-year-old biochemist Betty Mack Twarog. Twarog suspected that serotonin could have even more functions. She speculated that it might even be found in the brain.

Though Page was skeptical, he gave the young biochemist a laboratory. This proved to be a wise decision. In 1953 Twarog demonstrated that serotonin was to be found in mammalian brains—including human ones. Serotonin has a role to play in a range of different mental functions, such as appetite, sleep, aggression, impulsiveness and sexual desire. But above all it is important in anxiety and depression.

This sparked heated research activity, not least among pharmaceutical companies, who caught the whiff of money to be made. Would serotonin make it possible to alter humans' emotional state and make them less depressed and anxious? It was an opportunity that no one could afford to miss. Their labors soon bore fruit, and after a few years there were several medications available on the market that affected serotonin levels, but which also affected a number of other substances in the brain. When it became clear that these substances often had side effects, research was funneled toward developing medications that affected only serotonin levels. In the late 1980s a preparation was launched that came to be known as SSRIs.

Describing SSRIs as a commercial windfall is an understatement. The medications not only became commercial successes compared to other medicines; they have become some of the most sold products in history, full stop.

You may argue that we have always risked feeling low in the pecking order, which is of course true, but not by façades as perfect as the ones we are met with today. As if being constantly bombarded with our friends' filtered posts weren't enough, thousands of influencers—who get paid to promote their fantastic lives—set our bars for comparison unattainably high. Every other minute we come up against actual reminders that there is someone smarter, better-looking, richer, more popular or more successful than us, which inevitably leads us to feel like we are constantly being pushed down the pecking order—and in turn to risk feeling down.

At heart, the reason why we never stop evaluating our position in the hierarchy stems from the fact that our brains want to avoid loneliness. To protect ourselves from being ousted from the group, our brains are constantly asking themselves things like: *Do I fit in?* and *Am I good, smart, funny or beautiful enough to belong*? Today these questions are posed in an entirely different environment than the one our brains evolved for. In the same way that our craving for calories developed over hundreds of thousands of years in a calorie-strapped world—with devastating repercussions now that calories are much more readily available—our urge to compare ourselves to others evolved in a world in which we lived in small groups. When that instinct is transplanted into a situation that offers countless ways to feel inadequate, it can have consequences for our emotional lives. Precisely what these consequences will be isn't possible to say just yet, as research into how social media affects us is still in its infancy. However, a number of studies do suggest that young people who spend more than 4–5 hours per day on social media are less satisfied with themselves and feel more anxious and depressed. Still, the exact effect of social media has been hard to study, partly because social media companies have not wanted to share their research findings. In autumn 2021 it was revealed that Facebook's own researchers had warned that Instagram (which is owned by Facebook) was aggravating body image issues in one-third of all teenage girls. They also discovered that in teenagers who had reported having suicidal thoughts, 6–13 percent of all cases could trace their negative thoughts to Instagram. Facebook not only ignored these warnings; they also concealed them from the public.

But it's important to note that we all react differently to social media, and *not all of us* run the risk of feeling low as a result. The people who run the greatest risk of harm are more neurotic individuals (i.e., those who react particularly strongly to negative stimuli). The same is true of passive users of social media who simply scroll through others' posts without communicating in return. So what does this mean for us? Bearing in mind that we are descendants of not only the most calorie-craving, angst-ridden souls but also people who were absolutely desperate to belong, we can probably assume that some hours of daily comparison to other people's "perfect" lives will send a signal that the brain interprets as our being lower in the pecking order. As this risks making us feel down, it's probably wise to limit how much we expose ourselves to that signal. Limiting our use of social media (one unscientific suggestion is to give it one hour per day, max) is just as concrete a tip on how to hack our brain as taking deep breaths when we feel intense anxiety.

The loneliness epidemic

Every now and then we hear warnings that we are on the verge of a loneliness epidemic. From a wider historical perspective, there is reason to believe that this is true. There is a broad consensus among historians that for almost all of human history we lived in small groups of a few dozen individuals—a few hundred at the very most—who would have had close contact with each other and met daily. A persistent pattern among contemporary hunter-gatherers is that they devote 4–5 hours each day to hunting and gathering—in short, they do not have 40-hour weeks. The rest of their waking hours are spent with each other. If these people's lives are representative of how our ancestors lived, there is no doubt that our ancestors spent less time working, had closer social bonds and saw friends and relatives considerably more than we do. So yes, from a longer-term perspective—centuries and millennia—we probably have become lonelier, but whether that is true over a timeframe of decades is still up for debate. Some studies suggest that this is the case—for example, the number of Americans who responded "zero" when asked how many very close friends they could count on if something were to happen has grown in recent decades. And data compiled from the Organization for Economic Co-operation and Development (OECD) revealed that loneliness among teenagers had increased in all OECD countries between 2003 and 2015.

But there are also studies that show that we feel neither more nor less lonely today. In addition, it is hard to make a true comparison across generational lines as our perceptions of loneliness change. Is loneliness to go two hours without communicating with another, or two days? There is no "correct" answer here, but wherever that line is drawn will affect how many people perceive themselves as lonely—which makes it difficult, if not nigh on impossible, to compare the perceived loneliness in today's 20-year-olds with the 20-year-olds of the 1960s or 1990s. Although there are considerably more lone dwellers today than there were 20 years ago—one of the biggest societal changes in recent decades is how many people live alone—that doesn't necessarily mean that we are lonelier. Being alone, as we said earlier, doesn't automatically mean being lonely.

In other words, from the perspective of a few decades we can't say for certain whether we are facing a loneliness epidemic. Should we then not care about the issue? I am one of those who think we *should* care. Even though we are still at the very outset of our understanding of how loneliness affects us, we do know that it risks causing both emotional pain and a whole host of illnesses. And just because we can't say for sure that loneliness is on the rise, it can of course still be a problem. If we want to prevent depression and anxiety, we would be wise to weigh in loneliness as a major risk factor, in the same way that we consider lack of physical activity, sleep problems, stress and alcohol.

As a doctor and a psychiatrist, it has often struck me that a number of those who seek help because they feel unwell—both physically and mentally—actually do so because they feel lonely. They need someone to talk to who will listen to them and make them feel less isolated, and they are apparently unaware that loneliness might be the problem. This isn't so strange. As our brains are constantly working to find explanations for our emotional states, I often suspect that an aching back or knee can be the brain's way of concretizing the emotional pain that comes from loneliness. The best way to treat such an ache can be to tackle your loneliness.

So, to summarize, we are wired to connect and our deep social needs are due to the fact that human connection has always been, and is still interpreted as, survival by our brains. Of course, it's up to you whether this chapter makes you call your parents or grandparents that bit more often, make a habit of regularly visiting someone who's lonely or put a little less time into meeting through a screen in favor of meeting in real life. With fairly modest efforts, we as individuals and as a society could probably make a big difference to overcoming loneliness in a lot of people. If everyone were to make an effort to try to help at least one person who is lonely, it wouldn't just affect that person's subjective well-being or reduce their risk of depression; it would also lower their risk of and improve their prognosis in a range of serious illnesses. The fact is, it would give more people a longer life.

CHAPTER 6

EXERCISE

Whatever the mechanisms by which exercise boosts the brain,
you'd have to be a flat-earther to discount exercise as a potential
means to prevent and treat mental health problems.

DANIEL LIEBERMAN, PROFESSOR OF HUMAN
EVOLUTIONARY BIOLOGY, HARVARD UNIVERSITY

ANYONE WHO WORKS with patients in a healthcare setting will sooner or later start to see patterns. We get a sense for who will have good outcomes and whose will be less good. Now, we shouldn't extrapolate too wildly from these patterns—after all, they could just be coincidence, or us tending to remember the cases that confirm our own biases. But around the year 2010 I started noticing that patients who exercised and sought help for their depression didn't come back. After the odd follow-up visit, I would rarely see them again. This made me wonder whether exercise has an antidepressant effect. When I looked into the research, I discovered, to my great surprise, that this is the case. The last decade has seen a multitude of studies on treating depression with physical activity. However, the studies that surprised me the most, and which I also feel are the most important, look at how depression can be prevented and how physical activity can help us to reduce our risk of becoming depressed.

What does a bicycling test have to do with the risk of developing depression?

If you were to cycle as fast as possible for six minutes and then grip a handle for all you're worth, do you think it could say something about your risk of developing depression in the next seven years of your life? Ten years ago I would have found it extremely unlikely that my hand strength or performance on a test bike could have anything to do with whether I would get depressed in the future. Instead I would have guessed at other risk factors, such as losing my job, getting dumped or having a loved one fall sick. The tightness of my grip? Not a chance.

In the UK 150,000 study participants were asked to perform these two simple tests of fitness and hand strength and answer a number of questions on possible problems with depression and anxiety. When the questions were repeated seven years later, certain participants felt better than before, while others felt worse. In fact, some of them felt so much worse that they met the criteria for depression. Interestingly enough, there was a link between the changes in how they were feeling and the results of the cycle test seven years before—namely, the risk of depression appeared to be lower in those who were physically fit. Or to give more detail: for those who were physically fit, the risk of depression was halved and there was also a reduced risk of anxiety. Similarly, hand strength was linked to a lower risk of depression and anxiety symptoms, though the impact wasn't as obvious as that of cardiovascular fitness.

So the risk of depression appears to be lower in those who are in good shape—but let's now play devil's advocate. People who are in good shape are often healthy, seldom smoke, drink less alcohol and are more careful about what they put inside themselves. It could just as easily be another lifestyle factor that is in fact making the difference. To counter this, the researchers adjusted their results for age, smoking, education and income. The pattern remained. They then tried removing those who had been struggling with depression and anxiety at the start of the study and ran the numbers again. Nothing changed.

As you know, there is no clear line between depression and "normal" blues, so the results could have been caused by where that line was drawn. The researchers therefore tried different thresholds for what was considered depression. Yet again, the same pattern emerged. No matter how they looked at the data, the study indicated that those who were physically fit ran a lesser risk of becoming depressed. This is just one of a number of different studies that strongly suggests that physical activity can reduce the risk of depression. Still, looking at one or another study will never offer the best illustration of the current knowledge—even if the studies are so large as to comprise 150,000 people (in research, a good rule of thumb is "*one* study is *no* study"). Instead, we need to compile many different studies and perform what is called a "meta-analysis."

The research into how physical activity affects depression is actually now so exhaustive that in 2020 a meta-analysis of several meta-analyses was published (i.e., a meta-meta-analysis). The findings? Physical activity does indeed counteract symptoms of depression. The impact varies based on how the study was conducted, and spans from low to high. Given all the alarming reports on mental illness in young people, one might wonder if the same applies to this age group in particular. Yes, it does. One meta-meta-analysis that was presented in 2020 showed that exercise reduced the risk of depression in children and young people, with a moderate effect overall. And in the elderly? The same pattern there, too.

Accelerator and brake in one

Let's take a closer look at *why* exercise has such a powerful impact on how we feel. As we have previously seen, long-term stress is a risk factor in depression. The body's most central stress system is called the HPA axis, which can be traced tens of millions of years back in history. It is common to basically all vertebrates—including humans, apes, dogs, cats, rats, lizards and even fish.

The HPA axis is not one single organ but three different areas in the body and brain that communicate with each other. The first is the **h**ypothalamus (the "H" in HPA), which sends signals to the **p**ituitary gland (the "P") at the base of the brain, which in turn sends signals to the **a**drenal glands (the "A"). The adrenal glands then secrete the hormone cortisol, which mobilizes energy. For example, our cortisol levels rise in the morning to give us enough energy to get ourselves out of bed. But cortisol levels also rise in the case of stress. From H to P to A, cortisol is secreted when we get stressed. This may sound simple enough, but in practice the HPA axis is incredibly complex and contains several so-called feedback loops that mean it can brake itself. You see, when cortisol levels rise, activity in the hypothalamus and the pituitary gland is subdued. As a result, the cortisol applies its own brakes, and in doing so acts as both the body's stress hormone and its own "antistress hormone." It is almost like a car with just one pedal for both accelerating and braking, where if you hit the accelerator too hard the car will start to brake.

One of the most important discoveries in psychiatric research is that activity in the HPA axis often changes in depression. It is revealing that what is arguably the most important biological finding relating to depression comes from *both* the body and the brain, as the HPA axis spans the two. In most cases, the activity in the HPA axis increases during depression—i.e., cortisol levels are too high. Most treatments for depression, including medication, have a normalizing effect on the HPA axis (with different antidepressants affecting different parts of the axis), but medication isn't the only thing that normalizes it. Physical activity does, too. An overactive HPA axis is actually calmed through physical activity, but only in the long term. In the short term, exercise—particularly high-intensity training—increases activity in the HPA axis, as physical activity per se is a stressor on the body. So, when you go out for a run, the cortisol levels in your blood rise, but after the run they drop back to lower levels than before and remain there for up to a few hours. This contributes to the calm we often feel after exercise.

If you exercise regularly for a few weeks, the activity in the HPA axis will slowly start to wind down—and not just in the hours after the workout, but more generally. This is because the HPA axis has several different brakes. Two that are particularly important are the hippocampus, better known as the brain's memory center, and the frontal lobe, i.e., the part of the brain behind the forehead that is the seat of thought-related faculties such as abstraction and analytical thinking.

Both the hippocampus and the frontal lobe are strengthened by physical activity. In fact, the hippocampus gets physically bigger from exercise, and in the frontal lobe more small blood vessels are formed, expediting the supply of oxygen and the removal of waste products. This all enhances the brain's internal stress brakes, and, as if that wasn't already enough, exercise also improves the HPA axis's ability to stop itself, as it becomes more sensitive to its own activity. In other words, the braking ability improves in the pedal that serves as both accelerator and brake.

Exercise—the opposite of depression

As we saw in a previous chapter, depression is an umbrella term for a range of different conditions that can be caused by diverse neurobiological processes. Besides an overactive HPA axis, depression has been linked to inflammation in the body, which we also discussed earlier. It has also been linked to low levels of the neurotransmitters dopamine, serotonin and noradrenaline, and to low levels of the brain's own "fertilizer," brain-derived neurotrophic factor (or BDNF). Depression is also associated with altered activity in the insula (the part of the brain inside the temporal lobes, which is important in feelings) and increased activity in the amygdala.

These mechanisms, which are not mutually exclusive, can have a greater or lesser effect in different people. In reality, it isn't possible to say whether someone who is depressed is suffering from too little dopamine, an overactive amygdala or too much inflammation. But when it comes to exercise, that doesn't really matter, because no matter what the cause of the depression, physical activity often appears to be the exact opposite!

Exercise increases levels of dopamine, serotonin and noradrenaline, and also of BDNF. Over time, exercise also has an anti-inflammatory effect. This is because it takes energy to move, and that energy is in part diverted away from the immune system, which becomes less active. This may not sound like such a good thing, but since chronic inflammation is often caused by an overactive immune system— which exercise is able to calm—it *is* a good thing in this case. Exercise also speeds up the formation of brain cells in the hippocampus and normalizes the HPA axis. The list goes on, but I think you get the picture. From a biological perspective, it is hard to think of any one thing that is more diametrically opposed to depression than exercise. Another way of understanding the antidepressant effect that exercise has on us is to consider how our feelings are created. As you remember, feelings are formed when the insula combines your sensory impressions with what is going on inside your body. Thus, the brain uses both external and internal signals as ingredients when whipping up an emotional state.

Exercise strengthens all the organs and tissues in the body. Blood pressure, blood sugar and lipoproteins are stabilized, the lungs' maximum oxygen uptake improves and the heart and liver are given a boost. All of this means that the brain receives different—and better—signals from which to create feelings, increasing the likelihood that those feelings will be of pleasure and not discomfort. The fact is, exercise appears to be one of the most important things we can do to avoid depression.

Cause and effect

But let's put these neurobiological mechanisms to one side for a moment and once again assume the role of devil's advocate. In both New York City and Chicago, homicide numbers increase when lots of ice cream is sold. Does this mean that we should suspect the ice cream of making us aggressive and bloodthirsty, and lay the blame for the murders on their producers?

No—this is of course extremely unlikely. A more likely explanation is that we eat more ice cream when it's hot. We also happen to spend more time outdoors and drink more alcohol in this weather. More people spending more time outside while under the influence brings an increased risk of violence. Consequently, the weather affects both ice cream consumption and the number of murders, without the two having anything to do with each other.

So how can we be sure that there isn't something that affects both our risk of depression and how physically active we are? Perhaps exercise and a lower risk of depression have no more to do with each other than ice cream sales and homicides.

As if that wasn't enough, there is yet another challenge to navigate if we are to find out whether physical activity actually protects against depression. Studies into this very subject tend to be organized in roughly the following way: one group of test participants will be assigned cardiovascular exercise, while another will be assigned an activity that doesn't raise the heart rate, such as stretching. After a few months of regular exercise or stretching, the groups will be examined to see if there is any difference in how they feel. This is the same method used in the development of pharmaceutical drugs, where one group is given the medication and another group sugar pills. The problem is, when researching the mental impact of exercise, there is no good equivalent to sugar pills. After all, someone assigned exercise can see what they are doing and therefore guess that they are expected to feel good—they might even have read about one of the many studies I have already mentioned. So how can we know that this isn't a classic case of the placebo effect—that participants don't just feel better because they are expected to?

There's another snag: to be able to draw any conclusions that aren't just sheer luck, hundreds or thousands of people must be monitored for several years so that enough time will elapse for them to get depressed. American researchers decided to tackle all of these problems and sources of error by turning to genetics. You see, your risk of depression is up to 40 percent determined by your genes. Similarly, how much you exercise is to some extent influenced by genes—some people just have more spring in their step than others.

If people whose genes make them more likely to be more physically active are rarely depressed, it's a sign that physical activity truly does offer protection. If the genetic tests are then combined with exercise data and psychological tests, there is the possibility of drawing some interesting conclusions. For example, one could investigate if those who have multiple genetic risk factors for depression but exercise regularly are as depressed as they "should" be, statistically speaking. If this all sounds complicated, it's because it is. The method is called Mendelian randomization and it's one way of separating statistical links (such as ice cream and murders) from causal links (alcohol and murders). Mendelian randomization requires a large number of study participants, which these researchers had—over 200,000. But they faced yet another problem. When reporting how much we exercise, we have a tendency to overestimate, so the researchers decided to use pedometers, which give more objective data.

Finally, there was a chance to find out once and for all whether exercise reduces the risk of depression or if it is all just a placebo. The results, presented in one of the most prestigious psychiatric research journals in early 2019, couldn't be clearer: physical activity protects against depression and *cannot* be dismissed as a placebo. If every day you swap 15 minutes of sitting for 15 minutes of running, your risk of developing depression drops by 26 percent. If you instead walk for one hour, the reduction is exactly the same. As we can see, cardiovascular exercises such as running appear to be around four times as effective as walking. If you run for more than 15 minutes, or walk for more than an hour, your protection increases.

However advanced this study was, the researchers still decided to take the analysis one step further in order to be really sure. They did one more study in which they used a group of individuals who had a high genetic risk of depression. The high-risk individuals were monitored for two years, and during this time some of them did in fact become depressed. However, depression was less common among those who exercised. It did happen, but it was much rarer. The researchers' summary is unequivocal:

> Our findings strongly suggest that, when it comes to depression, genes are not destiny and that being physically active has the potential to neutralize the added risk of future episodes in individuals who are genetically vulnerable.

So we can in fact say for sure that depression can be both treated and prevented through exercise.

However, just because the risk is reduced doesn't mean it drops to zero. A reduced risk means just that—it is not zero risk. Nor does it mean that someone with depression should be accused of being unhealthy.

That the pedometer doesn't distinguish between whether you have walked to the store, mowed the lawn or trained for a marathon is important. All that matters is the movement itself. Even though cardio-vascular exercise is around four times more effective, at the end of the day it's the *number* of steps that helps to protect against depression, not where, when or how you take them. From a perspective of improved mental health we therefore have to expand our concept of exercise far beyond what goes on at the gym, soccer field or running track.

How many cases of depression could be prevented?

So, physical activity does give us an extra layer of "mental padding" against depression, but sadly this is gradually being thinned out. In the Western world we take on average 5,000–6,000 steps per day. Studies of communities that still live as hunter-gatherers, combined with analyses of 6,000–7,000-year-old skeletons, suggest that our ancestors walked 15,000–18,000 steps per day. For optimal functioning, our bodies and brains are most likely calibrated based on that number. In other words, we appear to be taking just one-third of the steps we have taken throughout the vast majority of human history.

The number of steps taken has not only shrunk from a long-term historical perspective but also in the shorter term. In Sweden the percentage of the population that is in such bad shape that it poses a health risk has risen from 27 to 46 percent since the mid-1990s. To meet the criteria of a "health risk," someone must be unable to sustain a brisk walk for over 10 minutes without a break. In young Swedish people, only 22 percent of boys and 15 percent of girls (aged 11–17) achieve the daily hour of physical activity recommended by the World Health Organization. There are good reasons to suspect the situation is no better in the US. The American Heart Association estimates that 60 percent of American children do not have healthy cardiorespiratory fitness. In other words, when it comes to modern-day exercise, we're in pretty bad shape.

Given that exercise protects against depression, we have therefore lost one of our main defenses against it. Which raises an interesting question: how many cases of depression could be prevented if we exercised a little more? This is exactly what researchers in the UK attempted to calculate, using data from 34,000 participants who were followed over the course of 11 years. Since many factors can affect each other in depression, it is difficult to dissect the role that each individual factor plays, so these results should be viewed as rough estimates rather than exact figures.

The researchers concluded that, had participants exercised for *just one hour per week*, 12 percent of depressions could have been prevented. Even children and young people appear to see good effects from relatively modest effort. Using pedometers, researchers followed the activity of just over 4,000 children and young people aged between 12 and 16, and a few years later the same participants were asked some questions on depression. It emerged that each additional hour of movement per week as teens was linked to a 10 percent drop in the scale of their depression symptoms at 18.

Anxiety and physical activity

Let's now turn our attention to anxiety. As we saw previously, the best way to describe anxiety is as "preemptive stress." Anxiety and stress are essentially the same reaction—an activation of the HPA axis—with the difference being that stress relates to a *concrete* threat, while anxiety relates to a *potential* one.

Because the HPA axis shifts up a gear in cases of stress and anxiety, and is stabilized through exercise, physical activity should in theory lead to less anxiety. So is that the case? In 2019 a meta-analysis explored a number of studies in which participants with different types of anxiety were assigned either exercise or another form of treatment. It turned out that cardiovascular exercise protected both children and adults from anxiety—particularly in the case of post-traumatic stress. Another meta-analysis that was published in 2020 examined 18 different studies. Every one of them showed that physical activity protects against anxiety, and that the type of exercise pursued matters less than the movement itself. Everything made a difference, be that swimming, walking, running on a treadmill, spinning or doing cardiovascular exercise at home.

In study upon study, meta-analysis upon meta-analysis, we see that those who exercise have less anxiety. The important thing is not *how* they exercise, but *if* they do. Those who suffer from panic attacks experience fewer of these when they exercise regularly, and when attacks do occur they are less intense. For those who suffer from social phobias, socially evaluative situations become less threatening. And those who have post-traumatic stress disorder experience less intense discomfort around flashbacks and elevated alertness. But, as with any other treatment for anxiety, such as therapy or medication, not everyone sees such positive effects from exercise. For some it works fantastically well, while others don't notice a huge difference. But the *average* effect on anxiety is good, just as it is for depression.

However, when it comes to preventing anxiety, one thing is important: increasing the heart rate. It would appear that the body gradually learns that a heightened pulse is not the same thing as a looming catastrophe—like my patient who had a panic attack on the subway—but is instead followed by lower cortisol levels, endorphins and a sense of well-being. In this way, it is possible to prevent the vicious circle of misinterpretations that seem to trigger a panic attack. Someone who is out of shape and has panic attacks or any other form of severe anxiety must therefore build up their training regimen slowly. Start with brisk walks for a month or two. Then jog slowly for a while and gradually increase the pace. If you are unfit and jump into exercise, your brain may misinterpret your increased heart rate as a sign of danger, which can at worst trigger an anxiety attack. Conversely, when you gradually intensify your workouts, slowly but surely you will notice the anxiety fade. It won't happen overnight; more like from one month to the next.

All forms of anxiety are reduced

As a doctor I can prescribe exercise, and whenever I have prescribed it to patients with anxiety, I'm often met with surprise. "Exercise?" they ask me. How could that change their stress and anxiety about life, work or their loved one's illness—or, indeed, the anxiety they don't even know the root of? It isn't possible to say with 100 percent certainty why evolution has shaped us so that physical activity alleviates anxiety, but think of it like this: the HPA axis's job is to mobilize energy for the body's muscles in the face of a threat—i.e., stress—or when the brain thinks a threat *could* emerge—i.e., anxiety. And what, for millions of years, presented the greatest threats to us? In which situations was it important that our evolutionarily preserved HPA axis mobilize energy? Hint: it was hardly psychosocial stress from bills, deadlines and everyday plate-spinning. It's significantly more likely that the HPA axis was developed to tackle threats to our lives, namely from predators, accidents and infections.

Those who are in good physical shape have a better chance of escaping predators, beating an adversary in combat or recovering from an infection. Their HPA axis doesn't need to jump into top gear whenever a potential hazard emerges. Nor do they have to go into a panic at every real or potential threat. Their stress system—i.e., their HPA axis—can shift down a gear.

When our brain deals with everyday psychosocial stresses, it uses the same system that humans have historically used to deal with threats to our lives. That which protected us against historic threats—including physical fitness—also calmed our ancestors' stress systems. Given the fact that we are biologically unchanged since those days, our HPA axis is still calmed by good physical fitness, and as a result we are better equipped to handle modern sources of stress and anxiety. Put simply: exercise teaches the body not to react so strongly to stress—whatever the cause of that stress might be.

So how do we become aware of the calmed state in the HPA axis after exercise? Does my brain get a notification that pops up as a thought after playing soccer? *Congrats, Anders! You have exercised and now your cortisol levels are back to normal. You're in great shape and won't have any problems running away should there be a lion lurking in the bushes.* Hardly. Instead I experience it as a *feeling*! A feeling of calm, reduced anxiety and a greater confidence in my own ability. And that confidence will spill over into whatever currently happens to be making me anxious. One of the most important psychological discoveries about the impact that physical activity has on us is that it boosts our *self-efficacy*, which can be defined as "a belief in our ability to complete a task."

MORE PERSPECTIVES

Exercise is no panacea, but those rarely exist. Antidepressant medication offers good benefits for one-third of all people with depression, moderate benefits for another third and no benefits at all for the final third. Roughly half of all patients being treated with cognitive behavioral therapy see good results, while for the other half the effects are modest. Similarly, when it comes to physical activity, results vary from individual to individual. Some feel fantastic effects, while others struggle to notice any real difference. However, on average the impact is good. If a depression is severe or involves exhaustion, intense physical activity is of course out of the question. In that case, rest and recovery are what the body needs, alongside therapy and, often, medication.

HOW LITTLE EXERCISE IS NEEDED?

Instead of asking how *much* exercise is needed to protect against depression, we should actually be asking *how little*. The short answer is that just one hour of brisk walking per week has been proven to give some level of protection. If you look into the research, what's striking is that, in children as well as adults, those who have the most to gain are those who go from doing nothing to doing something—for example, starting to cycle to work or walk to school. But more than that is of course even better, and so one might wonder what level is needed for maximal effects. A number of major, well-conducted studies suggest that between two and six hours of cardiovascular exercise per week is optimal. This is a wide range, but most studies lie closer to two hours than six. More than six hours of exercise per week appears to offer no additional protection.

Better belief in our own ability

Jättestenskolan is a primary and lower-secondary school of around 600 pupils just outside of Gothenburg, Sweden. In the early 2010s only every third pupil here completed their compulsory schooling with a pass in every subject. In an attempt to buck this trend, the school's head teachers, Lotta Lekander and Jonas Forsberg, decided to put research into action. Pupils normally had physical education (PE) twice a week, but Lekander and Forsberg wanted to see what would happen if they exercised every school day. The school therefore introduced half-hour sessions of physical activity for the three days when pupils didn't have PE lessons. The sessions were compulsory and were held in the gymnasium, and to avoid eating into other lessons they took place outside the usual timetable, meaning the school week became slightly longer. To avoid grade-related stresses, the sessions were not led by pupils' normal PE teachers, and participants were given a wide range of activities to choose from. The main thing was to increase the heart rate to 65–70 percent of its maximum for 30 minutes. No competing, no need to perform, just getting the heart rate up. The result? Two years on, the number of school leavers who passed in every subject had almost doubled.

When I first read about this school, I thought it sounded too good to be true. But when I looked into it some more, I learned that, in addition to the increase in physical activity, the school had also implemented a number of other changes. New staff members had been brought in, and the children's abilities and needs were being evaluated more systematically than before. So what role did the exercise play? To find out, I decided to visit the school while filming the Swedish popular science TV series *Your Brain*. Lekander and Forsberg gave me a warm welcome and told me that, although they couldn't give me a precise figure for the effect the exercise had had—their focus was on implementing practical changes, not conducting a research study—they believed that the "pulse sessions," as they called them, had been the single most important factor in giving pupils a boost. Interestingly, it wasn't the effect on grades that both head teachers were eager to discuss, but the fact that the pupils were feeling so much better. According to Lekander and Forsberg, pupils were less stressed and anxious, and they had also gained in confidence.

Lekander and Forsberg's impressions tally with what researchers in Chile also observed. Over a short space of time, Chile has come up against some major challenges with lifestyle diseases like diabetes and cardiovascular disease, and researchers wanted to see if it was possible to turn this around through lifestyle changes. They created a program in which young people from more disadvantaged areas were given the chance to take up running, basketball, volleyball, aerobics or football. The aim was for participants to find a form of exercise that they enjoyed, not to compete. At the end of the 10-week-long program it turned out that exercise had worked wonders for the young people's fitness. But something else had happened, too: they had become calmer, less anxious and had seen a boost to their self-esteem. Exercise enhances *self-efficacy*, particularly in children. Not only do they gain confidence in their athletic abilities, they also gain confidence overall—even in theoretical subjects. This is confirmed by a number of studies, including one major survey from The Public Health Agency of Sweden, which showed that physically active children are more satisfied with life and less stressed.

"Born to avoid starvation"

Here we are faced with a mystery: if physical activity boosts our self-confidence and makes us more satisfied with life, if it protects us from depression, subdues anxiety and stress, turns down our emotional thermostats and, on top of all that, fortifies every organ in the body, why has nature planted within us the urge to choose Netflix and chill over the running track? Why does our brain resist doing something that is so clearly good for it, with the result that almost everyone wishes they exercised more than they actually do? To understand this paradox, we need to bear two things in mind. First, the brain may be evolved for exercise, but its main purpose is survival; and second, throughout almost all of human history, starvation has posed a huge threat to our lives. Calories were a rare luxury that we did our best to immediately pounce on.

In recent decades more and more of us have gained constant access to as many calories as we want—it's just a matter of opening the fridge or popping to the store. But because evolution moves slowly—measuring time in millennia rather than decades—our brain has not yet adapted to this. Out on the savanna, the brain would be screaming: "Save me from starvation—guzzle all the calories you can find!" and that's exactly what it continues to scream as we buy our groceries. When presented with the candy aisle, our brain reacts exactly the same way it would have done had we been lucky enough to happen upon a gigantic tree loaded with fruit: "Jackpot! Wolf it down now!" Historically we could never get enough calories, and as a result we weren't equipped with a "stop" button for our calorie cravings. When this perpetual craving—developed over millions of years in a calorie-poor world that constantly had us on the brink of starvation—is transplanted into a world of unlimited calories, it isn't hard to predict the result. We eat. And eat. And eat. There is no end to how much we want to consume, and in this light our huge problems with obesity and Type 2 diabetes are not in the least surprising. What was once a survival mechanism is now a trap, as there is no longer any limit to how many calories we can get.

The amount of energy the body has available isn't only a question of how much food we eat but also of how much energy we expend—and exercise, as we know, takes energy. This is why we are lazy by default. In the same way that the brain wants us to guzzle down all the calories in the candy aisle, it also wants us to stay on the sofa and avoid burning unnecessary calories. You may be thinking that someone who is overweight has energy to spare, so why should their brain still want them to relax? The answer is that throughout the course of history we have almost never been overweight. There may have been a handful of pudgy emperors, pharaohs, kings and queens, but they were very much the exceptions.

For over 99.9 percent of our time on earth we have not had the luxury of excess pounds around the waist to dig into whenever food was scarce, which is why the body and brain have never developed defense mechanisms to say: "You've got more energy than you need—get outside and run off a few pounds so you won't get a heart attack in 30 years." Humans have never carried excess weight before; the majority never even reached an age where one would typically suffer a heart attack.

Today, excess weight and obesity have enormous repercussions for our health, while starvation in the developed world is extremely rare. Throughout almost all of human history, the exact opposite was true: excess weight was a non-problem and the looming threat of starvation a massive one. As a result, evolution developed not just one but a whole host of defense mechanisms to combat starvation. If we start losing weight, we feel hungrier. In addition, our basal metabolism (the amount of energy our body expends at rest) drops and nutrient uptake from our intestines increases. These mechanisms have one and the same function: the body is attempting to maintain its weight, as it perceives the lost kilos—be they excess weight or not—as a threat of starvation. While these mechanisms helped our ancestors to avoid starvation, they are a pretty effective wrench in the works when it comes to our attempts at dieting.

Just as we have evolved to seek out calorie-rich foods to escape the risk of starvation, we have evolved to seek relaxation, to save valuable calories wherever possible. In short, we're *supposed* to be lazy. Our ancestors would think we had a screw loose if they found out we were running ourselves sweaty only to arrive back at the same spot, or lifting heavy objects into the air just to put them down again. To them, voluntarily blowing our energy on something as unproductive as jogging or lifting dumbbells would be just as stupid as chucking food down the drain.

We're *supposed* to be lazy. Our ancestors would think we had a screw loose if they found out we were running ourselves sweaty only to arrive back at the same spot.

One sign that the concept of "exercise" would likely have been absurd to almost all previous generations comes from the hunter-gatherers who are still alive today. Of the 15,000–18,000 steps that they take daily, almost every single one has a specific purpose. Contrary to what one might think, these tribe members don't jump from one activity to another. In actual fact they spend most of their day seated, often together, and devote only 4–5 hours per day to hunting and gathering. So it's entirely natural that you and I, like contemporary hunter-gatherers, would rather flop on the sofa than lace up our running shoes.

Hack evolution!

The past decade has seen a number of unexpected discoveries come to the fore that reveal that physical activity improves not only the way we feel, but our mental faculties, too. In one study, students were asked to listen to a sequence of words through headphones. One group listened to the words while walking, another group while seated. When they were tested 48 hours later, it turned out that the ones who had been walking remembered 20 percent more words. Other studies show that physical exercise boosts concentration and creativity. For example, one study showed that the ability to brainstorm improved by over 50 percent in the hour following exercise.

When I first read about these experiments, I was surprised. For me, the concept of "brain training" simply brought to mind sudokus, crosswords and puzzle apps. How could physical activity have a greater effect on mental faculties such as memory, concentration and creativity than these cognitive tools?

The likely explanation is that the brain is the organ in the body that consumes the most energy, and, as with all other organs, it evolved to be as energy-efficient as possible. It will therefore only function *as well as it needs, in order to function.* For most of human history, it was when we were in motion that we needed our mental faculties the most. With movement we came to see new environments and gain sensory impressions that we had to remember. Hunting was when we would most need concentration and problem-solving skills. Even the other part of the hunter-gatherer lifestyle, the gathering, is mentally taxing. When moving through terrains, gatherers would need their full concentration to scan their surroundings for something edible, all while keeping an eye out for potential threats and possible escape routes. The margin for error was small, and if they found nothing to eat, then starvation would often be no more than a week or two away. All of this meant that their mental faculties had to be on top form.

Had the brain evolved for today's world, our mental faculties would be sharpest in front of a computer. But computers have only existed for two generations, and that is far too little time for us to have been able to adapt. As a consequence, the fact that physical activity sharpens our mental faculties offers a way for us to "hack" evolution. When we run on a treadmill or take a brisk walk, we trick the brain into amping up our mental faculties and can thereby use them in the way that suits us—the only limit is how long we can keep up the pace!

For me, learning that there is a logic behind our contradictory feelings toward exercise has been an important insight. I know that biological forces that have been honed over tens of thousands of generations are pulling me to the sofa, but I also know that the same forces have honed my brain to both feel and work better if I get moving. When exercise feels like too much of an uphill struggle, I sometimes tell myself not to let my genes—even less, evolution!—control me. I'm the one who calls the shots! I would be lying if I said these thoughts get me in my running shoes every time, but occasionally they do the trick.

Smart—but not wise

We have used our smart—but not always wise—brains to exclude unnecessary exercise. This is because we are lazy by nature, but while this was a strategy that worked brilliantly for hundreds of thousands of years, in modern society it has become a death trap. The World Health Organization estimates that every year 5 million people die early because they don't get enough exercise. By this calculation, it is likely that in 2020 as many people died due to a sedentary lifestyle as died of Covid-19.

By now our society has pushed convenience to the max, as electric scooters and food deliveries to our doors have helped to eliminate those last few steps from our lives. But we are learning that we have lost something vital along the way—when it comes to the risks not just to our physical health, but also to our mental health. I believe that we have to start finding smart ways to build exercise back into our lives. And that doesn't have to have the slightest thing to do with sports or performance. It might just mean starting to walk or cycle to work and taking the stairs instead of the elevator. Do anything that can become a habit. Ideally it should be something you do without thinking, in the same way that you brush your teeth without giving it a great deal of thought.

You may find the inactivity of modern life scary. But there is another way you can look at it: as a font of enormous potential. If we want to make a serious attempt not just to treat but also to prevent a whole host of physical ailments, as well as the mental health problems that so many people appear to be suffering from, physical activity is a treasure trove of untapped potential to draw from. If you exercise very little, then you are to be congratulated: all that treasure still awaits you, and you will be one of the people who enjoy the very best effects. The biggest impacts on mood, tolerance to stress and mental faculties are observed in those who go from doing nothing to doing a little.

Why did we forget the body?

You are not alone if the role the body plays in preventing anxiety and depression comes as a surprise. Judging by the reactions to my book *The Real Happy Pill*, which looked at how exercise boosts the brain, it is clear that many people have underestimated the role the body plays in their state of mind. Almost every day someone comes up to me and tells me how the book has changed their life. The majority of them say that they have started exercising and that it has made them feel better. A few encounters I will never forget: one was when a man in his mid-30s came running up to me at Stockholm's Arlanda Airport. He told me that he grew up in a war-torn region and that his post-traumatic stress from that period was at times so difficult to bear that he had considered taking his own life.

After reading the book he had taken up running—cautiously at first, then gradually stepping it up. As his anxiety melted away, he managed to reduce his alcohol intake. In the end he wasn't sure which of the two had made the greatest difference—running or cutting back on alcohol—but without the calming effect that the running had on his anxiety he would never have been able to tackle his alcohol problem. He was feeling better than he had in his entire adult life, and his only complaint about *The Real Happy Pill* was that I hadn't written it ten years earlier!

Of course, we should be cautious about drawing conclusions from reactions to a popular science book, but it's striking to me that hundreds of people have told me the same thing—that before they read the book they had dismissed the effect exercise has on their emotions as "fluff." I have wondered why they felt that way before reading *The Real Happy Pill* and think it may be down to the fact that in Western philosophy we traditionally separate body and soul. A long list of influential thinkers from Plato onward have described a soul that lives outside of the body and brain. Such a division between body and soul lends itself well to a belief in a "ghost in the machine"—that there is something more than the brain within us, such as a spirit or soul. This thought is, of course, appealing—it's nigh on impossible to conceive of the fact that our innermost feelings play out within an organ that looks like a bunch of squished sausages.

Increasingly, if perhaps slightly reluctantly, people have started to accept that feelings, thoughts and experiences do occur in the brain after all, and that its convolutions contain no spirits, souls or ghosts. In doing so, we have abandoned the division between body and soul, and instead applied that division to body and brain.

Yet that division is artificial. Brains don't whiz around the world in bell jars, separate from the body. No brain has ever existed without a body. The fact is, the brain didn't develop to think, feel or make us conscious, but to steer and control the body. To quote the distinguished neuroscientist Lisa Feldman Barrett: "As bodies got bigger and more complex during evolution, brains got bigger and more complex."

Brain and body are extremely closely linked, and in this book I have described a few recently uncovered examples of this link—such as the brain receiving information from the immune system, or the way it uses both internal and external stimuli to create feelings. As they are clearly visible and measurable, these external stimuli—sensory impressions, or what's going on at work, school and in our social lives—have been all too easy to fall back on when trying to explain our feelings and why we get depressed or anxious. However, the internal stimuli from the body are more difficult to capture, as they are by definition subjective. But research reveals that the role they play in our well-being is just as profound.

In other words, it isn't only possible to influence our feelings, depression and anxiety by therapy or by "balancing" the brain through medicine. Our physical condition is also more important than most people think. If I may speculate, I believe that research is only just beginning to deconstruct this artificial division between body and brain. As this division disappears, we will start to view depression, anxiety and human well-being not only from a *psychological* perspective, but from a *physiological* one, too. And it is in this very light that we should view physical activity.

CHAPTER 7

DO WE FEEL WORSE THAN EVER?

It was the best of times, it was the worst of times.

CHARLES DICKENS, *A TALE OF TWO CITIES*

IN MY LATE TEENS I started taking an interest in history. But this wasn't just an interest in Renaissance or medieval history, or even the cradle of civilization in Egypt and Mesopotamia; I was interested in the history of *our species*. Of how an insignificant, furless African ape, a mammal among many others, came to be the dominant creature on earth. I read everything I could get my hands on and remember being particularly surprised by the vast disparities between what killed our ancestors then and what kills us now.

Some years later, when I was studying to be a doctor and interning at Karolinska University Hospital, Sweden, I came face to face with these disparities in real life. Virtually no patients were being treated for illnesses that we humans have historically died from. No one was tussling with death from smallpox or malaria; no one was paralyzed by polio. It is a fantastic tribute to modern medicine that we have curbed, and even eradicated, some of history's worst and most deadly diseases. But then it hit me: how many of these patients would have been in the hospital had they lived like our ancestors? The patient with Type 2 diabetes, whose sky-high blood sugar had left him in a coma, would hardly have been there. Type 2 diabetes is caused, among other things, by high blood pressure and obesity, both of which were probably extremely rare among our ancestors. The same went for the patients who had suffered a heart attack, for which obesity, smoking and Type 2 diabetes are all risk factors. On the ward there were also a few patients who had suffered a stroke. They probably wouldn't have been there either, I guessed, as high blood pressure is the most significant risk factor in strokes.

When, later on in my training, I was on a rotation in the psychiatric ward at the same hospital, I was struck by the same thoughts. This time it was harder to guess how many people would have been admitted had they lived the way our ancestors did. Several people on the ward had been diagnosed with the psychotic disorder schizophrenia, and I suspected that they would probably have had this condition anyway. Schizophrenia is to a large degree hereditary, and surprisingly little has happened to our genes since our days on the savanna. The same was true of the patients who had the most severe forms of bipolar disorder, once termed "manic depression," which is also largely a hereditary condition.

But would the majority of the ward's patients—those who had been admitted for depression and anxiety—have been there had they lived the way our ancestors did? I realized that the question I was really asking was: do we feel worse than ever before?

Of course, it is extremely tricky to speculate on earlier generations' emotional lives; brains don't fossilize and our ancestors didn't leave us any psychological evaluations. However, it is clear that they were severely put to the test. We know that half of them died before they reached their teens. That means that the majority of adults lost at least one child. So, were as many of them depressed as we are? To make a qualified guess, we can study those who live as hunter-gatherers today. However, in this context, making a few odd visits to an exotic location and asking people to fill in a questionnaire won't cut it; researchers must be accepted by the community and follow its people over a matter of years. Which is exactly what anthropologist Edward Schieffelin did when he spent over a decade with the Kaluli of Papua New Guinea. He witnessed both pain and suffering, but despite their extremely challenging living conditions, in his interviews with the 2,000 tribe members he could only find a few who were depressed, and those tended to suffer only mild symptoms.

The same conclusion was reached by James Suzman after living with the Bushmen of the Kalahari for two decades. Depressions as we know them did occur, but they were unusual. A number of other anthropologists who have studied people in pre-industrial social structures, including the Hadza people in Tanzania and the Torajan people in Indonesia, have come to the same conclusion: few are depressed. What is striking is that modern hunter-gatherer living conditions are, as they were for our ancestors, very difficult. Almost half of the children die before reaching puberty, which is of course devastating for the parents. Yet although they mourn their lost children deeply, they rarely get depressed.

However, it would be wise to exercise caution before extrapolating too wildly from Suzman's, Schieffelin's and other anthropologists' experiences, as they are not trained in diagnosing depression. In addition, depressed tribe members could have concealed their problems, and we can't say with any certainty that today's hunterer-gatherers are representative of how we lived historically.

Still, the findings raise an interesting question: could something in the tribes' lifestyle protect against depression? Or we can flip the question on its head and ask ourselves: is there something in *our* lifestyle that makes us prone to depression?

Country life

This was the question that American researchers wanted to clear up when they embarked on a study of 657 women living in societies with different degrees of modernization. One group lived in rural Nigeria, another in urban settings in the same country, another in rural Canada and yet another in major American metropolises. The women were asked a long list of questions about how they were feeling, how well they slept, whether they had any difficulty concentrating, if they felt tired, lacking in energy, restless or indecisive or whether they had poor self-confidence. The questions were based on the criteria for depression found in the Diagnostic and Statistical Manual of Mental Disorders (DSM), the bible of psychiatric diagnoses.

The responses showed that, the more modernized the society was, the more people showed symptoms of depression. Women in rural Nigeria appeared to enjoy better mental health than those who lived in Nigerian cities, who in turn felt better than the women in rural Canada. Those who appeared to feel the worst were the women who lived in major US metropolises. This pattern was particularly apparent in women under the age of 45. But here too we should be cautious about the conclusions we draw. It isn't clear that the women were comparable. After all, we migrate based on the lives we want to lead. If people who are ambitious and anxiety-driven are more likely to move from the countryside to, say, Manhattan in an attempt to remedy their faltering self-esteem by making a career in the Big Apple, the city will soon be full of anxiety-driven people. Meanwhile, there will be fewer anxiety-driven individuals in the countryside. Comparing a randomly selected New York dweller with a randomly selected provincial American therefore runs the risk of comparing apples with pears. The same may apply when comparing women in rural Nigeria with women who live in big-city Lagos. Those who have certain personality traits tend to move to the cities, while others move away from them.

Although researchers had a psychiatrist review the questions so that they would be interpreted in exactly the same way by participants in the US, Nigeria and Canada, linguistic differences may still have had an influence. In addition, there may have been cultural differences at play in how we express ourselves when it comes to our emotions. In some societies, people describe their symptoms of depression as physical complaints; saying that your back hurts can be a way of saying that your soul hurts. But even with all these possible sources of error, the study still suggests that women in less-developed countries at least don't feel any *worse* than us, which means there is yet another reason to believe that something in their lifestyle protects them against depression. We will come back to explore what that might be shortly.

Do we feel worse than we have in decades?

However interesting these findings are, I still struggle to shake the feeling that these women are slightly too far removed from our lives, so let's take a look at the incidence of depression a little closer to home and in a contemporary timeframe. There has been an explosion in prescriptions of antidepressant medication in the United States in recent decades. Today, one in eight adults is prescribed such medication, but the US doesn't top the chart—in the UK, Iceland and Portugal these figures are even higher. The upward curve in most age groups and in economically affluent countries is so steep that it risks provoking the same condition it describes.

So do we feel worse? Well, we still can't say for sure, as simply looking at how many people are being prescribed medication isn't enough. After all, this could be due to the fact that nowadays people are more likely to seek help, or that doctors keep their prescription sheets closer to hand. We can get a loose idea of how well-being has changed over the course of some decades by looking at studies in which the same questions about depression and its symptoms have been posed to large numbers of randomly selected people at different points in time. One such survey, which provides data from 600,000 Americans, shows that depression actually did become more common in the US between 2005 and 2015. This was particularly true among teenagers, where there was an increase of just over 40 percent.

A French study revealed that there were more people with depression in 2005 than in the early 1990s, but that this increase was fairly slight. In a comprehensive Australian study, it was estimated that 6.8 percent of the population were depressed in 1998, compared to 10.3 percent in 2008—a roughly two-fold increase over a decade. When German researchers reviewed findings from 1997 to 2012, however, it turned out that just as many people were depressed in 2012 as in 1997.

In Japan it has been gauged that the number of people with depression increased by 64 percent between 2003 and 2014. However, the main cause for this appears to be that more people are seeking help, so the increase doesn't necessarily mean that more people are depressed. The World Health Organization stated that the number of people with depression increased globally between 2005 and 2015—but it is worth remembering that in the same time period the population of the world grew by 13 percent.

I understand if this barrage of figures and statistics may be confusing—it certainly was for me. The studies don't point unequivocally in one particular direction. Some show that more people in the world today are depressed, while others suggest only a slight increase, if any. The waters are further muddied by how difficult it is to compare studies from different time periods. After all, there's no blood test, gene or X-ray examination that can tell decisively if you have depression. The studies are all built around asking questions about how someone feels, and, unlike X-ray imaging, blood and genetic tests, words can change meaning. If every ten years we were to ask 1,000 Americans if they often feel down, their response would reflect whatever "down" means right then. However, it may have meant one thing in the 1970s and mean a completely different thing today. I need look no further than myself when I was in secondary school in the 1990s. Back then, the word "psychiatry" made me and, I'm sure, many others think of straitjackets and padded rooms, and as a result many people didn't dare seek psychiatric help. Having more people talking about mental illness today is a good thing, but it makes it hard to compare today's findings against surveys conducted in days gone by.

Trying to find out if more people really are depressed today seems an almost hopeless task, but I decided not to give up and to do some more digging. Having read numerous studies, papers and reports, I came to the conclusion that the majority of the most well-conducted, meticulous studies, which employed questions that don't tend to change in meaning over time, and which also measured objective symptoms in a large number of individuals, suggest that there is no significant difference, or that we feel slightly better but that the increase is small. The exception is in teenage girls, where there is much to suggest that depression and anxiety have in fact risen in the past decade, as we saw in Chapter 5.

Beyond this, it is impossible to say whether more people are depressed today than 20 or 30 years ago. The same is true when it comes to diagnoses of ADHD and autism. The most exhaustive studies suggest that, although the number of diagnoses has risen sharply, this isn't due to a rise in incidence. This doesn't necessarily mean that too many people are being diagnosed today, but that *more* people probably should have been diagnosed 20 years ago.

However, what we can say is truly remarkable is that the number of cases of depression clearly has not reduced! It isn't just that many more people are getting medication and therapy now than they were a few decades ago; the medical developments of recent years have also been extraordinary. I have touched upon the fact that the twentieth century saw huge advances in treating infectious diseases, and that the positive trajectory for medical developments didn't let up. Once we started surviving infections in greater numbers, heart attacks and cancer started taking the most lives, but even in treating these diseases we have seen vast improvements. The fatality of heart attacks has fallen substantially, in Sweden by more than 50 percent since the turn of the millennium. In the 1980s four in ten people were still alive ten years after their diagnosis of myocardial infarction; today that figure is seven in ten. Advances in medicine have helped us to live longer. Globally, the average life expectancy has increased by seven years since 1990. In Sweden, Europe and Japan it has increased by five years in the same time period, so by two months each year and in the US by one year. And we're not just adding more years to our lives; we're adding more *healthy* years.

Economic and medical development have gone hand in hand. Sweden's gross national product has increased by almost 100 percent since the 1990s; we have become twice as wealthy. And we aren't alone there. To name just a few, Germany's economy grew by 80 percent between 1997 and 2012, and the US economy almost tripled between 1990 and 2018.

But despite these fantastic medical and economic developments, we don't appear to be feeling substantially better mentally. It's striking that more people aren't reflecting upon this, as the main promise of every ideology, religion and political party is to create well-being and make us feel better. If you are wondering what the economy has to do with how we feel, try asking a hard-headed capitalist why we should bother with economic development at all. They will tell you that it's so that we can enjoy life. And if you naively counter by asking why we should enjoy life, you will be told that obviously it's so that we can *feel good*. But apparently we don't. Given how good we have things, we actually feel pretty rough.

Despite the fantastic medical and economic developments of recent decades, we don't appear to be feeling any better mentally.

Why are we still in the same place?

That we don't appear to feel a lot better today than we did 20 years ago, despite our various advances, can be demoralizing. It seems that we will always feel the way we feel, no matter what medical and economic progress is made. Any attempt to change that is pointless. But as a psychiatrist, I refuse to believe this is the case. Through therapy, exercise and medication I have seen enough people not only recover from depression and anxiety, but also learn how to prevent them, which is why I believe that the pursuit of mental health is anything but hopeless! While the question of whether we feel better or worse than we did 20, 200 or 20,000 years ago is certainly interesting, the key is what action we can take in the here and now.

Of course, we can't vaccinate against mental health problems—I hope by now you'll agree that that's unrealistic—but we can nevertheless feel much better. How we go about this is a complex question that must be considered from multiple points of view. One important perspective that is too often forgotten is the paradoxical findings of Suzman, Schieffelin et al. that depressions are uncommon in modern-day hunter-gatherers, even though they live in materially difficult conditions. There is something about their lifestyle that protects them from depression, or, conversely, something about our lifestyle that makes us more susceptible to it. I believe that this "something" is, above all, physical activity and spending time with other people. Those who still live as hunter-gatherers often walk 15,000–18,000 steps per day and are physically active for two to three hours, one hour of which is intensive. They also have strong social bonds and live in close proximity to each other. Both of these factors protect them against anxiety and depression. Added to this is the fact that they rarely smoke, are less exposed to environmental toxins and don't eat as much processed food as we do. They also work less and live in more equal societies.

What if . . . ?

The precise role played by each of these factors is of course difficult to quantify. What is clear, however, is that physical activity and reduced loneliness play an important role, and in this regard some relatively small changes could help many people to avoid ending up in a situation where they need treatment for mental health problems. Just imagine if we exercised a little more, upped the number of steps we walk each day to, say, 10,000, and prioritized meeting up in real life slightly more often. Imagine if everyone who didn't feel lonely put aside one hour each week to support someone who did. What would happen then? We can perhaps get a rough idea from the studies I described earlier, in which researchers calculated that 20 percent of all depressions are caused by loneliness, and that 12 percent of all depressions could be avoided if we exercised more. From a global perspective that would mean the number of people with depression could drop by up to 100 million.

And we would probably have much more to gain than a reduction in depression.

Modern-day hunter-gatherers who reach the Western world's retirement age are exceptionally healthy. Excess weight and obesity are very uncommon; high blood pressure, too. Type 2 diabetes is so rare that it has been difficult to get a figure on it at all—we simply can't find anyone affected. The blood vessels in 80-year-old members of the Tsimané tribe in Bolivia are in the same shape as those of 55-year-old Westerners. All of this is made even more noteworthy by the fact that none of them are prescribed medication to lower their blood pressure or lipids. No one checks their glucose levels or invites them in for health checks. They don't even have access to running water and electricity.

Despite the absence of all forms of health care and the most basic facilities, modern-day hunter-gatherers are in exceptionally good physical shape, and the same seems to be true of their emotional well-being. Depression is unusual, even though they have access to neither therapists nor antidepressants, and even though the majority of all adults have lost at least one child. We can only speculate as to how our physical and emotional health would look in the West if we were suddenly to lose access to all health care, antidepressants and therapy, and if most adults had lost a child.

Almost two decades' work as a doctor has made me realize that, when it comes to human health and emotional well-being, we won't reap the greatest rewards through spectacular research or by giving psychotropic drugs to an even greater percentage of the population. We will probably see the greatest results from something as old-fashioned and low-tech as sharing knowledge and motivating people to take an extra walk or visit their loved ones a little more often.

This also applies in economic terms. For 13 years psychiatrist Thomas Insel led the National Institute of Mental Health, the largest funder of psychiatric research in the world. His leadership saw a mind-boggling 20 billion dollars awarded to research. In 2017, Insel summarized the impact of the billions invested:

> When I look back on that I realize that while I think I succeeded at getting lots of really cool papers published . . . I don't think we moved the needle in reducing suicide, reducing hospitalizations, improving recovery for the tens of millions of people who have mental illness.

We can do all the research in the world into the brain and develop the most cutting-edge expertise, but if it doesn't reach out and change our lives, then ultimately it's meaningless. I am not saying that psychiatric research is pointless—nothing could be further from the truth. But when it comes to our physical and mental health, it's important not just to look ahead to innovative new technology and spectacular research findings. Equally important is looking back at our evolutionary history and sharing knowledge that offers a deeper understanding of how depression and anxiety can be prevented, and in doing so promoting behaviors that mean we avoid ending up in a situation in which we need psychiatric assistance. We can't rewind to a life on the savanna, but we can take lessons from the historical conditions that have shaped us.

But if we have not evolved to feel happy, and if much of what we view as illness could be defense mechanisms, who should we help? Where do we draw the line between normal emotional swings that are part and parcel of life and something that should be diagnosed? When does feeling down become depression? What is shyness and what is a social phobia? There are no simple answers here, beyond the fact that you should seek help if your life is being limited by your state of mind. We have successively lowered the threshold for what suffering we are willing to accept, and in my book that is progress. In Sweden, the fact that more people are seeking help and are receiving medication and therapy has helped to reduce suicide figures by 30 percent since the 1990s. It seems clear, then, that speaking openly about mental illness saves lives and alleviates suffering. I am convinced that this openness solves more problems than it creates. But it isn't completely unproblematic, and in the next chapter we are going to take a closer look at a trap that we should be careful not to fall into.

CHAPTER 8

THE DESTINY INSTINCT

Whether you think you can, or you think you can't—you're right.

HENRY FORD

I knew I'd end up somewhere like this sooner or later. It was only a matter of time before I got depressed. Several of my relatives have depression, so I guess I have too little serotonin in my brain.

I HAVE HEARD SO MANY of my patients say something along these lines. Some say that they are suffering from a lack of serotonin, others dopamine. A few say that they have "bad" genes. The problem isn't that they are describing their symptoms of depression or anxiety in biological terms—even if, as we know, it's hardly as simple as having "too little" serotonin. The problem is that they see their problems as something predestined.

We as humans have something of a soft spot for believing that things cannot be changed and that events are inevitable. This is a psychological idiosyncrasy that is entirely natural. When you think back to your childhood, you probably remember a world that was in many ways different than today's—without smartphones, the internet or even computers. But you are an exception: for almost all of human history, not that much changed during a lifetime. The world that people grew up in was broadly the same as the one they grew old in—if they were lucky enough to reach old age, that is. The brain, and with it our mental faculties, adapted over hundreds of thousands of years to expect that the world around us won't change. Hans Rosling, the distinguished professor of global health, called our inclination to believe that the world "is what it is" our "destiny instinct." The destiny instinct not only fools us into believing that certain continents and countries are sentenced to follow a particular progression; it also fools us into believing that we can't change and are sentenced to feel a certain way forevermore. I believe that, if we view our emotional lives through the prism of biological terms like "too little" serotonin, an "overactive" amygdala or "bad" genes, this destiny instinct risks infiltrating our minds.

Lost control

Let's say you decide to do a genetic test. You pay your fee and get a little package through the mail with a tube that you spit into and then send back. Three weeks later you get an email to say that the results are ready. Not without some trepidation you log in and read that 2.2 percent of your DNA comes from Neanderthals. Your roots on your mother's side can be traced back to a woman who lived in the Middle East 11,000 years ago. She was your maternal grandmother's great-great-great- (× 450) grandmother. It's fascinating stuff, at least if you—like me—are inclined to nerd out on these things, though perhaps not life-changing. You scroll down to the "health risks" section. Here it states that you have a 30 percent higher risk of developing cardiovascular disease. This doesn't make for fun reading, but neither is it a big surprise, as a number of relatives on your father's side have had a heart attack.

You are now faced with the question of what to do with the information you just received. You can say that your genetic risk of heart attacks is what it is and can't be changed. However, there are risk factors that you can influence, and you decide to insist on annual health checks. You get a gym membership, buy some running shoes and banish cheese puffs and cookies from the pantry. If you manage to stick to your new healthier lifestyle, your genetic test may just have saved you from a heart attack—and thereby helped to extend your life by several years.

You scroll on through the health risks and read that you also run an increased risk of developing an alcohol dependency. This does come as a surprise, as to your knowledge no one in your family has had alcohol problems. But no one becomes an alcoholic just because of their genes—it takes alcohol, too—and you can steer clear of that. Wine bottles can be poured down the drain and New Year can be marked with alcohol-free bubbly. Then your genetic risk will never have any consequences. All's well that ends well. But is it really that simple? Unfortunately not.

In one study, researchers told participants that they carried a gene that increased their risk of developing an alcohol dependency. This wasn't true—none of them carried such a gene—but the point of the study was to find out how participants would react to hearing that they ran an increased genetic risk of alcohol abuse. As it happened, the participants who were given this false information found it *harder* to cut out alcohol. They started to see alcohol problems as an inevitable fate. Their destiny instinct had reared its head.

Your genetic test also shows that you run an increased risk of becoming depressed. As with heart attacks and alcohol abuse, you can say that your genetic risk is what it is and can't be changed, but there are still risk factors that you can influence. You can start exercising, prioritize sleep, take care to avoid excessive stress and spend more time with your nearest and dearest. In which case the information might just have saved you from depression.

But in the same way that we find it harder to steer clear of alcohol if we find out that we carry a genetic risk of developing an addiction, information on our genetic risk of depression also appears to affect how we view our own resilience. When researchers told a group of people with depression that it was caused by something in their brain, the people became more pessimistic about their possibility of recovery. Their confidence in their own ability to manage their feelings shrunk and they felt that it would take more time for them to get better. "It makes no difference what I do, there's something wrong with my brain," appeared to be their reasoning. They were convinced the best treatment was medication. The same phenomenon was observed in a group of patients with generalized anxiety disorder. When they were told that their anxiety was caused by too little serotonin, they felt that their chances of ridding themselves of the anxiety diminished—their destiny instinct seemed to kick in.

It thus looks like a biological perspective on anxiety, depression and addiction that puts the stress on genes and misdosed neurotransmitters makes us perceive the conditions as inevitable. This can at worst lead to them becoming self-fulfilling prophecies. When our emotional lives are described in terms of dopamine, serotonin or the amygdala, we perceive them as being unchangeable. They become set in stone.

It may sound bleak that, when we realize our darker feelings have a biological basis, our destiny instinct threatens to cement them, but there is an effective antidote: knowledge. In one study, participants were shown a video clip that explained that, although genes do *affect* our risk of depression, they don't *determine* whether we will become depressed. The video stressed that the brain is more like modeling clay than porcelain. It is changeable—plastic—and how it works depends on how we live our lives. How much we sleep, whether we exercise, whether we are exposed to long-term and unpredictable stress, whether we see friends or go to therapy—everything affects how the brain works. The film was instructive in showing how things like exercise affect the chemistry of the brain and even change how the genes in our brain cells are used. After the video, participants felt less pessimistic and suddenly considered their chances of getting themselves out of depression to be improved. Perhaps you assume the film was unscientific and full of exaggerations. It wasn't. It presented the latest knowledge, and it was no long-winded snoozefest, but a seven-minute-long YouTube clip.

Knowledge about knowledge is the solution

We are currently in the midst of a scientific revolution. With every passing day we are learning more and more about how our mental faculties and feelings are created by the brain, and how the brain in turn is shaped by our DNA and external environment. Such knowledge can unlock fantastic potential in everything from health care to well-being and education, but it's important that it be presented in a way that does no harm. Research into genetics and the brain is not about certainties but likelihoods. The problem is that we humans often think in black and white as opposed to shades of gray. An "*increased* risk of depression" isn't the same thing as "*guaranteed* depression," but that's often how we can perceive it.

The point is, although research into the brain is moving at breakneck speed, our brains aren't actually going anywhere. They have remained basically unchanged for 10,000 years, and as a result we are more afraid of snakes and spiders than cigarettes and cars, and we view the world as static and immovable. Therefore, a swell of medical discoveries about how we operate "under the hood" will be handled by a brain that is poorly equipped to interpret statistical probabilities in medical research articles. To prevent all this new knowledge about the brain from making us see ourselves as more steered by our biology than we really are, we need to teach ourselves to think scientifically. This takes practice, but it isn't actually *so* hard. After watching that informative, seven-minute-long clip, participants had a greater confidence in their own ability to handle their emotional lives. And that confidence was still there six weeks after seeing the clip.

In other words, knowledge is the solution. And not just knowledge about *how* the brain works, but also knowledge about *why* it works the way it does. By teaching ourselves that the brain's most important task is to promote our survival—and that it adapted to do so in a highly precarious world—we realize that milder forms of what we call mental illness don't necessarily mean that we are sick, much less broken.

You are not your diagnosis

If we were to choose the single quality that most distinguishes humans from other animals, our gift for telling stories would not be a bad choice. Our brains are constantly engaged in trying to find an explanation for what we experience, and are constantly creating stories that make events fit together. They are especially on the lookout for a story that makes our lives coherent, that makes them understandable and predictable. A story that can not only explain the world but explain ourselves.

In my work I have occasionally seen a psychiatric diagnosis become that story. Certain people identify with their diagnosis and start to see themselves as "the sick person." The diagnosis becomes a sort of identity to them. This is a shame, because such identities are not just a way for the brain to make sense of our past, they become road maps for our future. It can thus become a self-fulfilling prophecy to see ourselves in this way—it triggers the destiny instinct.

Just because you feel a lot of anxiety in one period of your life, doesn't mean you will always feel that way.

Every time I meet a patient like this, I explain that both anxiety and depression can be a sign that the brain is working normally. In addition, everyone who experiences severe anxiety is different. Everyone who experiences depression is different. Humans are far more complex than any diagnosis can explain. A diagnosis doesn't communicate everything about you; you are *not* your diagnosis. I also usually point out that feelings change, too—and that is what they are supposed to do, as otherwise they would serve no purpose. This also applies to our darker feelings. Just because you feel a lot of anxiety in one period of your life, doesn't mean you will always feel that way.

CHAPTER 9

THE HAPPINESS TRAP

Brains don't react, they predict.

LISA FELDMAN BARRETT,
PROFESSOR AND RESEARCHER OF AFFECTIVE SCIENCE

BY NOW WE have devoted almost an entire book to exploring why the brain hasn't developed to feel happy but to constantly plan for the worst—anxiety—and occasionally withdraw as a self-defense mechanism—depression. So now it's time to flip the script and try to find out what makes us happy. Despite an increased academic interest in this question (this burgeoning research field is known as positive psychiatry), and "happiness" being one of the few words that have more Google hits than "anxiety"—902 million—it's difficult to delineate what it actually means.

Many people equate happiness with feeling positive. They view happiness as a constant state of pleasure and contentment, while in research happiness is often defined by how satisfied we are with the direction our life has taken. In this way, happiness can be seen more as having a long-term sense of purpose than constantly feeling great. If you agree with this definition and want to do your utmost to be happy, I think the best thing you can actually do is ignore happiness.

Yes, forget all about it! The less we care about it, the greater chance we have of finding it.

You see, the brain constantly tries to predict what is coming, then it maps what actually happens against these predictions. For example, let's say you step into your bathroom at home. Before doing so, your brain is already pulling up memories about the room and is therefore activated in a way that reflects the sensory impressions it expects to find. When you then step into the bathroom, what you see, hear and feel is mapped against your predictions. If the brain's forecasts match these impressions, you won't react, but if something deviates from your predictions, then you will stop short.

Our lives are made up of an endless string of comparisons like this, in matters both big and small, as our brains hold up what actually happens against their own predictions. When elderly British people were asked about their physical health in spring 2021, the percentage of people who considered themselves to be in good health had *increased* on the previous year. However, there isn't much to suggest that these people's health had actually improved during the pandemic year of 2020. On the contrary, there were good grounds to suspect that their health had deteriorated, given that in the UK over 100,000 people died of Covid-19 and the health system was so stretched that anything but the most urgent care often functioned worse than normal. So why would they have felt healthier? One possible explanation is that, in the light of daily reminders of illness and suffering, their bar for what they counted as good health had been lowered. As media reports of overburdened intensive care units and morgues fed into one another, they no longer considered an aching back, sore knee or recurring headaches as such a big problem. Their brains' predictions—against which they mapped their lived experience—had changed, and with that so did their views on their own health.

In such a way we are neurobiologically hard-wired to compare everything we experience to our own predictions and expectations, rather than to take an objective view on what happens. This may sound obvious, but even so, it can often go under the radar. When I studied economics, our professors would often open lectures by stating: "Mankind is a rational creature that always prefers more to less." As a doctor and psychiatrist, I have realized that this is completely wrong. We don't prefer more to *less*. We prefer having more *compared to our neighbors*. Our perception of how well our lives are going is based on how others' are. Your Audi feels fantastic until your neighbor pulls up in their new Tesla.

An unrealistic state

That we have evolved to map our every experience against our expectations is the reason why we shouldn't bother striving for happiness. As you have seen in previous chapters, feelings of well-being are supposed to be transitory or else they wouldn't fulfill their primary function of motivating us. The brain is constantly updating our emotional state based on the information it receives from our bodies and surroundings. That it should shut itself off in a positive emotional state so that we can always feel great is, from the brain's perspective, just as unrealistic as the banana on the kitchen counter keeping us full for the rest of our lives. We're just not built that way, but we are fooled into thinking that we are.

That we have evolved to map our every experience against our expectations is the reason why we shouldn't bother striving for happiness.

In 2015 Coca-Cola launched a huge marketing campaign. The drinks giant no longer encouraged us to "share a Coke" but to "choose happiness." The message this hammered into billions of people was that happiness is something we choose, and that not only *can* we be happy, we *should* be. Coca-Cola is far from the only brand that has tried to link its product to an unrealistic emotional state. Here are a few more examples: "Live happily ever after" (home insurance), "Happy starts here" (mustard), "Happiness shared" (food), "Help yourself to happiness" (a restaurant) and "Moments of happiness" (dairy products). These are just a handful of advertising slogans with the same subtext: happiness is an endless string of joyful experiences, and it's something we *choose*. If we don't feel happy, there's something wrong with us.

Through this slew and barrage of slogans, plus the 902 million Google hits, we are reminded that we both can and should be happy—that is to say, feel great every day. And so the brain maps our subjective experiences against a goal that is, in fact, unreachable; constant well-being is not a natural state for humans. If we allow ourselves to be bombarded by façades of happy, attractive and apparently harmonious people in tropical sunsets, our expectations of our own emotions will be unrealistically high. When our inner world then doesn't match these expectations—which no one's can—we become disappointed. Our advertising-informed, deeply unrealistic image of happiness thereby risks making us unhappy. And no, this isn't just speculation.

When study participants read an article that extolled the virtues of happiness before they watched a comedy, they were less happy after the film than those who had read an article that didn't mention happiness. One possible explanation is that the article about happiness raised participants' expectations, and with that came the hopes that the film would be side-splittingly funny. When it then wasn't as hilarious as the participants hoped, it became a disappointment.

When we have no expectations, we set the bar lower and an experience becomes level with, or higher than, our expectations, with positive results on how we view that experience.

Interestingly enough, it has emerged that the more money a country spends on advertising each year, the less satisfied its residents are with life two years later. This leads one to suspect that advertising does play a role in us setting our expectations of our emotional lives unrealistically high, resulting in disappointment and dissatisfaction. An advertising slogan that would put our expectations at a more realistic level—and that might actually have a positive impact on our well-being—would be: "It's OK to feel down sometimes." But that probably wouldn't sell all that many fizzy drinks, jars of mustard or home insurance plans.

Unlike most things that we strive for, where the chances of success increase with the more effort we put in, the opposite seems to be true of happiness. The more we chase happiness per se, the more we risk it slipping through our fingers. The single best piece of advice I can give someone who wants to be happy is to turn a deaf ear to all hollow advertising messages. Close every article or book and turn up your bullshit detector for every YouTube lecture that even mentions the word.

But besides ignoring happiness, is there nothing we can do to be happy? Here I hesitate to speculate, partly because what works for me won't necessarily work for anyone else, and partly because any attempt at advice is a slippery slope to a ditch full of fluffy, unverifiable clichés. But if I absolutely have to stick my head above the parapet, I believe that one of the most dangerous misconceptions in modern society is that happiness is made up of an endless stream of joyful experiences.

Admittedly, we have no idea how our ancestors viewed happiness (the word "happy" can be traced back to the fourteenth century and originally meant "lucky"), but it is extremely unlikely that the hunter-gatherers who roamed the African savanna believed that an endless stream of joyful experiences was what gave life meaning. For almost all of human history, our current vision of happiness would have been so absurd that it wouldn't even be a fantasy. Our obsession with happiness—and our misconception that happiness is the same as constant well-being—is only a few generations old, but since most of us have known nothing else, we can't see how strange and unrealistic it is.

For me, happiness is neither about striving for a constant bed of roses nor about playing down anything to do with our own discomfort. At the same time, I'm materialistic and comfortable enough to know I would be lying if I said that convenience and material factors don't play any role in it. They are undoubtedly important—for me and almost everyone else. The most constructive definition of happiness that I have heard is that it's a combination of positive experiences and a deeper insight into yourself; an insight into what you're good at and how these qualities can be used to help yourself and others, and in doing so to help you become a part of something greater than yourself. For most people, the penny finally drops when they find themselves not at their goal, but at a stage where they are working toward something that is larger than themselves. That is where they find what, for want of a better word, can be called "happiness." In summary, happiness shouldn't be viewed as a goal in and of itself, but as part of a greater context.

Happiness comes when we understand what's important to us in life and build from that; when we become part of something that we consider meaningful to ourselves and others. It isn't particularly surprising that most of us work this way. After all, our survival has depended on our ability to work together. Those who survived nature's gauntlet—and as a result became our ancestors—did it *together*. We didn't become the dominant species on earth because we were the strongest, fastest or smartest, but because we were the best at working together. That's why we suffer so acutely from loneliness.

When the Austrian psychiatrist and neurologist Viktor Frankl was asked how he managed to muster the spiritual strength to survive four concentration camps, including Auschwitz, he quoted the philosopher Friedrich Nietzsche: "He who has a *why* to live can bear almost any *how*." The things that are meaningful enough to create such a *why* are probably as numerous as there are people in this world, but one thing is sure: constant joy is not one of them. So don't chase happiness. Happiness is a byproduct that appears when you stop thinking about it and instead focus on something that feels meaningful.

AFTERWORD

I REMEMBER IT like it was yesterday. I was in my second term of medical school. The room was chilly, the air filled with a strangely pungent smell as a fan whirred in the background. But the autopsy room fell away when I looked down at what I held in my hands: a human brain. *It's all in here,* I thought. Everything the 84-year-old man whose brain I was holding had experienced. All of his memories, all of his feelings. Every moment of his life, from cradle to grave, was played out in something he never saw himself—the object that was now in my hands. I was holding what had essentially made a person's "me." I shuddered when I realized that I too have a brain and that it too contains everything I have ever experienced. My first day of school, dressed in an itchy, granddad-collar shirt; my teenage years; the time when 20-year-old me almost killed myself skiing in Chamonix. Even the experience of me holding the 84-year-old's brain was being created in my brain!

There was something mesmerizing about the fact that my entire life up to that point had played out in an organ that looked like a large walnut, had the consistency of tofu and weighed just a couple of pounds. I still can't get my head around it, despite having spent unhealthy amounts of time trying to. But the most important thing

I learned that day—the thing I remind myself and my patients of daily—is that the brain is an organ. And just like all the other organs on the table in the autopsy room, the brain has evolved to perform one task: survive.

The brain isn't the way it is by mere chance. It doesn't show us the world as it is. It doesn't let us remember events we experienced as they actually occurred. It doesn't let us see ourselves as we are. Far from it! The brain changes our memories. It works from the worst-case scenario and draws up disastrous situations. It occasionally fools us into thinking that we're more competent and social than we actually are, and sometimes into thinking that we're completely worthless. In reality it's no more than a machine for survival, full of bugs that, when viewed in an evolutionary light, often turn out to be smart functions.

The brain is no passive intermediary that anyone with an interest in human nature might as well skip. Quite the opposite! To learn about the brain provides a deeper understanding of human nature because it is within the brain that human nature, in the end, is created. Having said that, the brain cannot be seen in isolation. It is part of a complicated and dynamic system—the body—that it not only controls, but also receives information from. Any information that signals a threat, such as a risk of infection, isolation or a step down in the hierarchy, makes the brain create feelings of discomfort. These very feelings have resulted in behaviors that increased our chances of survival in the conditions we lived in for hundreds of thousands of years, and which we are still adapted for. If we believe that anxiety, depression and a desire to withdraw mean that the brain doesn't work—or is sick—we have forgotten that its primary function is survival.

"It's all in the head" is a phrase often said of depression and anxiety. When I was growing up, this meant that you were supposed to "pull yourself together"—which I doubt anyone has ever found helpful to hear. But later "it's all in the head" came to mean "too little serotonin in the brain." While this was a step forward—away from trivialization—it risked creating self-fulfilling prophecies. It's time to change "it's all in the head" to "it's all in the head and the body and is often a sign that everything is working entirely normally."

I believe that the reason we feel worse than we should, given how well we have it, is that we've forgotten that we're biological beings. I have written this book as a reminder of our biological foundations and to show how our emotional lives are shaped by "popping our hoods" and taking a look inside the engine of our souls. A book that tackles the major question of human well-being must, however, be selective, and for this reason I have consciously decided to focus on biology and the brain and not go into further detail about social explanatory models—not because inequality, exclusion, injustice and unemployment don't matter, but because we have a tendency to overlook our biology.

Besides highlighting two key influential ingredients in our emotions that many underestimate the value of—physical activity and loneliness prevention—I have refrained from giving too many tips or pieces of advice. Instead I have tried to present a way of observing yourself and your emotional life that I hope will make it possible for you to draw your own important conclusions, and which I know from experience can be both forgiving and dedramatizing. Still, I would like to offer a few pieces of advice, so in the next section I'll summarize my ten most important insights into seeing yourself from the brain's perspective.

MY TOP TEN INSIGHTS

You are a survivor. We have not evolved for health or happiness, but for survival and reproduction. Feeling great all the time is an unrealistic goal. We just aren't built that way.

Feelings are there to affect your behavior, and they are supposed to change. Feelings are generated when the brain combines what is going on inside you with what is going on around you. The body's internal state has a greater role to play in our feelings than most people think.

Anxiety and depression are often defense mechanisms. They are a normal part of human nature and do not mean you are damaged or sick. And they have absolutely nothing to do with shortcomings in your character!

Memories are—and are supposed to be—changeable! Talking about traumatic events in a safe space means that these memories shift and become less threatening.

Lack of sleep, long-term stress, a sedentary lifestyle and over-exposure to other people's photoshopped façades on social media risk sending signals that the brain interprets as looming danger or personal inadequacy. It then responds by telling you to withdraw and makes you feel low.

Physical activity protects against depression and anxiety. You are made to move, which is something we do too little of today. Still, laziness is normal!

Loneliness has been linked to a range of illnesses, but small gestures can make a big difference. A few close friends are probably better from a health perspective than a large number of superficial acquaintances.

Genes are important, but environment is often more so. Don't believe that something being genetically conditioned means it's inevitable. How you live your life affects how your brain works.

Forget about happiness! Expecting to always be happy is not just taxing and unrealistic—it can have exactly the opposite effect.

Most important of all in this book, if you feel mentally unwell, you should seek help. Mental illness is no more unnatural than pneumonia or an allergy. Help is there for you and you are not alone.

BIBLIOGRAPHY

1.Why do we feel so bad when we have it so good?

World Health Organization, "Depression," (September 13, 2021), https://www.who.int/news-room/fact-sheets/detail/depression

World Health Organization, "Depression and other common mental disorders: Global Health Estimates," (2017), License: CC BY-NC-SA 3.0 IGO

2. Why do we have feelings?

Diamond, J., *The Third Chimpanzee: The Evolution and Future of the Human Animal* (London, Hutchinson Radius, 1991)

EurekAlert!, "Penn researchers calculate how much the eye tells the brain," (July 26, 2006)

Feldman Barrett, L., *How Emotions Are Made: The Secret Life of the Brain* (Boston, Mariner Books, 2017)

Gozzi, A. et al., "A neural switch for active and passive fear," *Neuron* 67:4 (2010), 656–66. DOI: 10.1016/j. neuron.2010.07.008

Harari, Y., *Sapiens: A Brief History of Humankind* (New York, Harper, 2015)

3. Anxiety and panic

Bai, S. et al., "Efficacy and safety of anti-inflammatory agents for the treatment of major depressive disorder: a systematic review and meta-analysis of randomized controlled trials," *Journal of Neurology, Neurosurgery & Psychiatry* 91:1 (2019), 21–32. DOI: 10.1136/jnnp-2019-320912

Burklund, L. et al., "The common and distinct neural bases of affect labeling and reappraisal in healthy adults," *Frontiers in Psychology* 5:221 (2014). DOI: 10. 3389/fpsyg.2014.00221

Chippaux, J.P., "Epidemiology of snakebites in Europe: A systematic review of the literature," *Toxicon* 59:1 (2012), 86–99

Crocq, M., "A history of anxiety: from Hippocrates to DSM," *Dialogues in Clinical Neuroscience* 17:3 (2015). DOI: 10.31887/DCNS.2015.17.3/macrocq

Hariri, A.R. et al., "Neocortical modulation of the amygdala response to fearful stimuli," *Biological Psychiatry* 53:6 (2003), 494–501. DOI: 10.1016/s0006-3223(02)01786-9

Nesse, R., *Good Reasons for Bad Feelings: Insights from the Frontier of Evolutionary Psychiatry* (Boston, Dutton, 2019)

World Health Organization, ed., "Deaths on the roads: Based on the WHO Global Status Report on Road Safety 2015" (PDF) (official report) (Geneva, Switzerland, 2015) [accessed January 26, 2016]

4. Depression

Andrew, P.W. et al., "The bright side of being blue: depression as an adaptation for analyzing complex problems," *Psychological Review* 116:3 (July 2009), 620–54. DOI: 10.1037/a0016242

Bai, S. et al., "Efficacy and safety of anti-inflammatory agents for the treatment of major depressive disorder: a systematic review and meta-analysis of randomized controlled trials," *Journal of Neurology, Neurosurgery and Psychiatry* 91:1 (2019), 21–32. DOI: 10.1136/jnnp-2019-320912

Bosma-den Boer, M.M. et al., "Chronic inflammatory diseases are stimulated by current lifestyle: how diet, stress levels and medication prevent our body from recovering," *Nutrition & Metabolism* 9:1 (2012). DOI:10.1186/1743-7075-9-32

Eurostat, "Statistics explained. Cancer statistics." (August 2021)

Goldman, L., *Too Much of a Good Thing: How Four Key Survival Traits Are Now Killing Us* (New York, Little Brown, 2015)

Gruber, J., "Four Ways Happiness Can Hurt You," *Greater Good* magazine (May 3, 2012) https://greatergood.berkeley.edu/article/item/four_ways_happiness_can_hurt_you

Gurven, M. et al., "A cross-cultural examination," *Population and Development Review* 33:2 (2007), 321–65. DOI: 10.1111/j.1728-4457.2007.00171.x

Gurven, M. et al., "Longevity among hunter-gatherers: a cross cultural examination," *Population and Development Review* (2007)

Husain, M.I. et al., "Anti-inflammatory treatments for mood disorders: systematic review and meta-analysis," *Journal of Psychopharmacology* 31:9 (2017), 1137–48. DOI: 10.1177/0269881117725711

Jha, M.K. et al., "Anti-inflammatory treatments for major depressive disorder, what's on the horizon?," *The Journal of Clinical Psychiatry* 80:6 (2019). DOI: 10.4088/JCP.18ac12630

Quan, N. and Banks, W.A., "Brain-immune communication pathways," *Brain, Behavior, and Immunity* 21:6 (2007), 727–35. DOI: 10.1016/j.bbi.2007. 05.005

Raison, C.L. and Miller, A.H., "The evolutionary significance of depression in Pathogen Host Defense (PATHOS-D)," *Molecular Psychiatry* 18:1 (2013), 15–37. DOI: 10.1038/mp.2012.2

Riksarkivet (The Swedish National Archives), "TBC och sanatorier (TB and Sanatoria)"

Straub, R., "The brain and immune system prompt energy shortage in chronic inflammation and aging," *Nature Reviews Rheumatology* 13:12 (2017), 743–51. DOI: 10.1038/nrrheum.2017.172

Wium-Andersen, M.K. et al., "Elevated C-reactive protein levels, psychological distress, and depression in 73,131 individuals," *JAMA Psychiatry* 70:2 (2013), 176–84. DOI: 10.1001/2013.jamapsychiatry.102

Wray, N.R. et al., "Genome-wide association analysis identifies 44 risk variants and refine the genetic architecture of major depressive disorder," *Nature Genetics* 50:5 (2017), 668–81. DOI: 10.1101.167577

5. Loneliness

Berger, M. et al., "The expanded biology of serotonin," *Annual Review of Medicine* 60:1 (2018), 355–66. DOI: 10.1146/annurev.med.60.042307.110802

Cacioppo, J. et al., "The growing problem of loneliness," *Lancet* 391:10119 (2018), 426

Cole, S.W. et al., "Myeloid differentiation architecture of leukocyte transcriptome dynamics in perceived social isolation," *Proceedings of the National Academy of Sciences* 112:49 (2015), 15142–7. DOI: 10.1073/pnas.1514249112

Cruwys, T. et al., "Social group memberships protect against future depression, alleviate depression symptoms and prevent depression relapse," *Social Science & Medicine* 98 (2013), 179–86. DOI: 10.1016/j.socscimed.2013.09.013

Dunbar, R., *Friends: Understanding the Power of Our Most Important Relationships* (London, Little Brown, 2021)

Dunbar, R. et al., "Social laughter is correlated with an elevated pain threshold," *Proceedings of the Royal Society B* 279:1731 (2001), 1161–7. DOI: 10.1098/rspb.2011.1373

Folkhälsomyndigheten (The Public Health Agency of Sweden), "Skolbarns hälsovanor—så mår skolbarn i Sverige jämfört med skolbarn i andra länder" ("Health practices of schoolchildren—how schoolchildren in Sweden feel compared to schoolchildren in other countries") (May 19, 2020)

Kahlon, M. et al., "Effect of layperson-delivered, empathy-focused program of telephone calls on loneliness, depression, and anxiety among adults during the COVID-19 pandemic. A randomized clinical trial," *JAMA Psychiatry* 78:6 (2021), 616–22. DOI:10.1001/jamapsychiatry.2021.0113

Keles, B. et al., "A systematic review: the influence of social media on depression, anxiety and psychological distress in adolescents," *Int. Journal of Adolescence and Youth* 25:1 (2019), 79–93. DOI: 10.1080/02673843.2019.1590851

Masi, C. et al., "A meta-analysis of interventions to reduce loneliness," *Personality and Social Psychology Review* 15:3 (2010), 219–66. DOI: 10.1177/1088868310377394

McPherson, M. et al., "Social isolation in America: changes in core discussion networks over two decades," *American Sociological Review* 71:3 (2006), 353–75. DOI: 10.1177/000312240607100301

Meltzer, H. et al., "Feelings of loneliness among adults with mental disorder," *Social Psychiatry and Psychiatric Epidemiology* 48:1 (2012), 5–13. DOI: 10.1007/s00127-012-0515-8

Mineo, L., "Good genes are nice, but joy is better," *The Harvard Gazette* (April 11, 2017)

Ortiz-Ospina, E., "Is there a loneliness epidemic?," *Our World in Data* (December 11, 2019)

Provine, R.P. and Fischer, K.R., "Laughing, smiling, and talking: relation to sleeping and social context in humans," *Ethology* 83:4 (1989), 295–305. DOI: 10.1111/j.1439-0310.1989.tb00536.x

Tomova, L. et al., "Acute social isolation evokes midbrain craving responses similar to hunger," *Nature Neuroscience* 23 (2020), 1597–605. DOI: 10.1038/s41593-020-00742-z

Trzesniewski, K. et al., "Rethinking Generation Me: a study of cohort effects from 1976–2006," *Perspectives on Psychological Science* 5:1 (2010), 58–75. DOI: 10.1177/1745691609356789

Wells, G., Horwitz, J. and Seetharaman, D., "The Facebook files: Facebook knows Instagram is toxic for teen girls, company documents show," *Wall Street Journal* (September 14, 2021)

6. Exercise

Babyak, M. et al., "Exercise treatment for major depression: maintenance of therapeutic benefit at 10 months," *Psychosomatic Medicine* 62:5 (2000), 633–8. DOI: 10.1097/00006842-200009000-00006

Bridle, C. et al., "Effect of exercise on depression severity in older people: systematic review and meta-analysis of randomized controlled trials," *The British Journal of Psychiatry: The Journal of Mental Science* 201:3 (2018), 180–5. DOI: 10.1192/bjp.bp.111.095174

Choi, K.W. et al., "Assessment of bidirectional relationships between physical activity and depression among adults: a 2-sample Mendelian randomization study," *JAMA Psychiatry* 76:4 (2019), 399–408. DOI: 10.1001/jamapsychiatry.2018.4175

Folkhälsomyndigheten (The Public Health Agency of Sweden), "Psykisk hälsa och suicidprevention/Barn och unga—psykisk hälsa/Fysisk aktivitet och psykisk hälsa" ("Mental health and suicide prevention/Children and young people— mental health/Physical activity and mental health") (2021)

Harvey, S.B. et al., "Exercise and the prevention of depression: results of the HUNT cohort study," *American Journal of Psychiatry* 175·1 (2017), 28–36. DOI: 10.1176/appi.ajp.2017.16111223

Hu, M. et al., "Exercise interventions for the prevention of depression: a systemic review of meta-analyses," *BMC Public Health* 20:1255 (2020). DOI: 10.1186/s12889-020-09323-y

Kandola, A. et al., "Depressive symptoms and objectively measured physical activity and sedentary behavior throughout adolescence: a prospective cohort study," *Lancet Psychiatry* 7:3 (2020), 262–71. DOI: 10.1016/S2215-0366(20)30034-1

Kandola, A.A. et al., "Individual and combined associations between cardiorespiratory fitness and grip strength with common mental disorders: a prospective cohort study in the UK Biobank," *BMC Medicine* 18:303 (2020). DOI: 10.1186/s12916-020-01782-9

Netz, Y. et al., "Is the comparison between exercise and pharmacologic treatment of depression in the clinical practice guideline of the American College of Physicians evidence-based?," *Frontiers in Pharmacology* 8:257 (2017). DOI: 10.3389/fphar.2017.00257

Raustorp, A. et al., "Comparisons of pedometer-determined weekday physical activity among Swedish school children and adolescents in 2000 and 2017 showed the highest reductions in adolescents," *Acta Pediatrica* 107:7 (2018)

Schmidt-Kassow, M. et al., "Physical exercise during encoding improves vocabulary learning in young female adults: a neuroendocrinological study," *PLoS One* 8:5 (2013), e64172. DOI: 10.1371/journal.pone.0064172

Schuch, F. et al., "Physical activity protects from incident anxiety: a meta-analysis of prospective cohort studies," *Depression and Anxiety* 36:9 (2019), 846–58. DOI: 10.1002/da.22915

Tafet, G.E. and Nemeroff, C.B., "Pharmacological treatment of anxiety disorders: the role of the HPA axis," *Frontiers in Psychiatry* 11:443 (2020). DOI: 10.3389/fpsyt.2020.0044

Wegner, M. et al., "Systematic review of meta-analyses: exercise effects on depression in children and adolescents," *Frontiers in Psychiatry* 8:81 (2020). DOI: 10.3389/fpsyt.2020.00081

Winter, B. et al., "High impact running improves learning," *Neurobiology of Learning and Memory* 87:4 (2007), 597–609. DOI: 10.1016/j.nlm.2006.11.003

7. Do we feel worse than ever?

Colla, J. et al., "Depression and modernization: a cross-cultural study of women," *Psychiatry Epidemiology* 41:4 (April 2006), 271–9

Goldney, R.D. et al., "Changes in the prevalence of major depression in an Australian community sample between 1998 and 2008," *The Australian and New Zealand Journal of Psychiatry* 44:10 (2010), 901–10. DOI: 10.3109/00048674.2010.490520

Hollan, D.W. and Wellenkamp, J.C., *Contentment and Suffering: Culture and Experience in Toraja* (New York, Columbia University Press, 1994)

Nishi, D. et al., "Prevalence of mental disorders and mental health service use in Japan," *Psychiatry and Clinical Neurosciences Frontier Review* 73:8 (2019), 458–65. DOI: 10.1111/pcn.12894

Rodgers, A., "Star neuroscientist Tom Insel leaves the Google-spawned Verily for . . . a startup?," *Wired* (November 5, 2017)

Socialstyrelsen (National Board of Health and Welfare, Sweden). *Statistik om hjärtinfarkter (Heart Attack Statistics)* (2018)

Socialstyrelsen och Cancerfonden (National Board of Health and Welfare, Sweden, and the Swedish Cancer Society), *Cancer i siffror 2018 (Cancer in Figures 2018)* (2018)

Statistiska centralbyrån (Statistics Sweden), *Life Expectancy 1751–2020*

Sweden's National Board of Health and Welfare, Statistics on prescribed medicine in Sweden, February 28, 2022

World Health Organization, "'Depression: Let's talk' says WHO, as depression tops list of causes of ill health" (2017)

8. The destiny instinct

Feldman, S., "Consumer genetic testing is gaining momentum," *Statista* (November 18, 2019)

Lebowitz, M.S. and Ahn, W.K., "Blue genes? Understanding and mitigating negative consequences of personalized information about genetic risk for depression," *Journal of Genetic Counseling* 27:1 (2018), 204–16. DOI: 10.1007/s10897-017-0140-5

Lebowitz, M.S. et al., "Fixable or fate? Perceptions of the biology of depression," *Journal of Consulting and Clinical Psychology* 81:3 (2013), 518–27. DOI: 10. 1037/a0031730

Rosling, H., *Factfulness: Ten Reasons We're Wrong about the World—and Why Things Are Better than You Think* (New York, Flatiron Books, 2018)

9. The happiness trap

Frankl, V., *Man's Search for Meaning* (Boston, Beacon Press, 1947)

Torres, N., "Advertising makes us unhappy," *Harvard Business Review* (Jan–Feb 2020)

ACKNOWLEDGMENTS

An early draft of this book formed the basis of my *Summer on P1* radio show, and when that was received so warmly I decided to finish writing the book. But it would probably never have become a finished book were it not for a number of people whom I would like to send a huge thank-you to here.

Cecilia Viklund and Anna Paljak at Bonnier Fakta, for always encouraging me, offering constructive feedback and once again teaching me that the keyboard's most important key is "Delete." Erika Strand Berglund, for your dedication as a sounding board and for your uncannily precise tips about small changes that make for great improvements. Charlotta Larsson, Sofia Heurlin and everyone else at Bonnier Fakta, for helping to get the books out to readers in Sweden. Federico Ambrosini, Kimia Kaviani, Adam Torbjörnsson, Elin Englund and everyone else at Salomonsson Agency, for helping me to reach other countries, too. Gratitude to my US team at Penguin Random House: thank you to my editor, Sarah Curley; production editor Bethany Reis; Christina MacDonald, who Americanized the text; proofreader Hope Clarke; designer Emma Hall; compositor Kim Scott; and operations director and scheduling extraordinaire Meredith Snyder, for bringing the book to the US market.

I would also like to thank, in no particular order, the following people, who in many different and important ways have contributed to the book: Carl Johan Sundberg, Gustav Söderström, Jonas Pettersson, Otto Ankarcrona, Mats Thorén, André Heinz, Simon Kyaga, Tahir Jamil, Vanja Hansen, Björn Hansen, Desirée Dutina, Martin Lorenzon, Niklas Nyberg, Pontus Andersson, Daphna Shohamy, Karl Tobieson, Malin Sjöstrand, Anders Wallensten and the staff at the National Library of Sweden.

Finally, I would like to send my biggest thank-you to anyone who has read my books and in some way let me know that you appreciated them. That means more to me than any sales figures in the world!

INDEX

abuse 30, 34
addiction 144
adrenal glands 104
adrenaline 94
advertising industry 152–3
Africa 5, 53, 127, 154
age effects 103
aggression 95, 197
agrarian society 7, 9–10, 53
agriculture 9–10, 53
alcohol consumption 99, 103, 107–8
alcohol dependency 123–4, 143–4
alertness 6, 79, 112
Alzheimer's disease 61
amygdala 14, 142, 144
    and anxiety 36, 38–9, 42
    dampening the activity of 38–9
    and depression 106
    and memory 31
    and panic attacks 24, 28
analytical rumination hypothesis 70
ancestors 5–10, 7, 135
    causes of death 7, 127–9
    and depression 47, 50–3, 128–9
    and feelings 18
    and group living 78–9, 97–8

and happiness 153–4
and infection 52–4, 56
and inflammation 61
and laziness 119–20
and panic attacks 26
and satisfaction 19
and threat perception 114
anthropologists 129, 136
anti-inflammatories, natural 106
antibodies 57
antidepressants 46, 48, 131
    and anxiety 36
    clinical efficacy 114
    and cytokine blockers 65
    and the HPA axis 104–5
    and serotonin levels 92–5
    widely used nature of 2
anxiety 1, 20, 21–43, 138, 149, 158
    anticipatory 23
    biological view of 36, 38–9, 42–3
    and the body 123–4, 125
    and the brain 3, 27, 34, 36–40,
        42, 71
    and childhood trauma 40–1
    constant, low-level 21
    and depression 46, 48

anxiety—*cont.*
 and genetics 27, 41, 47, 144
 and the HPA axis 111–14
 and loneliness 84, 99
 as normal reaction 21, 35, 43, 147,
  158–9, 161
 and physical activity 36, 102–3,
  111–15, 117, 123–4, 162
 as "preemptive stress" 22, 111
 prevalence 2
 prevention 135, 136
 recovery from 135
 and serotonin 95
 severe 34–6, 128
 and shame 11
 and social comparison making
  96, 97
 and social media 96, 97
 and survival 11
 treatment 35–9, 42–3
 triggers 22
appetite 46, 95
arrhythmia 76
attention 16
attention deficit hyperactivity disorder
  (ADHD) 133
Auschwitz 155
Australia 132
autism 133
autonomic nervous system 37, 77–9, 81
avoidance behaviors 29, 35

bacteria 49, 55–7, 60–2, 65, 67
Barrett, Lisa Feldman 124, 149
behavior, and feelings 15, 19, 161
behavioral immune system 57
belonging, sense of 29, 81, 90, 97
Bergman, Ingmar 39
Biden, Joe 52
biology 159
 see also evolutionary biology
bipolar disorder 47, 128

blood pressure
 elevated 79
 high 94–5, 128, 137
body
 and depression 123, 125
 and emotional pain 99
 evolution 8
 and feelings 161
 and the HPA axis 104
 and loneliness 73, 76, 78
 see also brain-body connection
body fat 26, 62, 64
body image 97
body temperature, raised 60
Bolivia 137
brain 1, 3, 157–8, 159
 and anxiety 3, 27, 34, 36–40,
  42, 71
 capacity for change 36
 and childhood trauma 41
 control function 77
 and decision-making 17–18
 and depression 3, 46, 49, 57, 60,
  64, 66–7, 71, 106, 144–5
 and endorphin release 87–9
 and feelings 15–19, 107, 161
 "hacks" 38
 and the HPA axis 104
 and the immune system 58–9, 66,
  125
 and individual difference 16–17
 and inflammation 62, 64
 and information processing 15–16
 knowledge about the 146
 and laziness 118
 and loneliness 73, 76, 78–83,
  96, 99
 and memory 1, 20, 30–2, 158
 "normal" 17
 and overeating 118
 and panic attacks 25, 26–8, 34,
  113

Turn the page for a sneak peek at Dr. Anders Hansen's global bestsellers

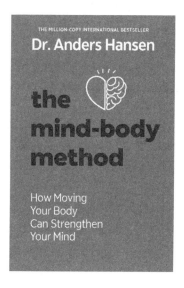

the attention fix

How to Focus
In a World That
Wants to
Distract You

Dr. Anders Hansen

Zeitgeist • New York

FOCUS—THE SCARCITY OF OUR TIME

The price of multitasking

The brain has an incredible ability to handle a wide range of processes in parallel, but there is one area in which our mental bandwidth is severely limited: our attention. We simply cannot focus on more than one thing at a time.

What we are actually doing when we think we are multitasking is jumping quickly between tasks.

When you are listening to a lecture while also writing an email—and feeling impressed by your own ability to do both at the same time—the truth is that you are switching quickly between the two. And while shifting focus may only take a tenth of a second, the problem is that your brain lingers on what you just did. When you turn your attention to your email, your brain will continue to dedicate some of its bandwidth to the lecturer. The same happens when you switch from writing emails to listening to the lecture.

That the brain has a transition period and lingers on what you were just doing is known in scientific language as "attention residue." When you think you are only spending a few seconds on your emails, the price is actually higher. It's not possible to say exactly how long this transition period lasts, but studies suggest that it takes several minutes for the brain to focus 100 percent on a task after a change of focus.

Not *everyone* is bad at multitasking, however. There are actually those who *can* do several things in parallel. They are a small group sometimes referred to as "super-multitaskers." It's believed that a few percent of the population have this trait. But for the vast majority, the brain *doesn't* work that way. Interestingly, women generally seem to be better at multitasking than men.

Your phone distracts even on silent

Both our concentration and our working memory seem to be negatively affected by trying to do several things at once. Now, you are probably thinking that this means we just have to turn off our computers and leave our phones on silent in our pockets. Unfortunately, it's not that simple. As you saw in the last chapter, cell phones have an almost unparalleled ability to attract our attention, and that doesn't seem to cease just because we put them down.

When the memory and concentration of 500 university students were tested, those who had to leave their cell phone outside the testing room performed better than those who had it on silent in their pocket. The test subjects had no idea that the presence of their

phone was affecting them, but the results spoke for themselves—
they were distracted merely by having it on their person. The same
phenomenon has been observed in several other studies. In one,
800 people were asked to perform a series of high-concentration
exercises on a computer. Afterward, it turned out that those who
had left their cell phone in another room performed better than
those who had it on silent in their pocket. To find out the results, it's
enough to read the title of the research report: "Brain drain: the
mere presence of one's own smartphone reduces available cognitive
capacity."

Japanese researchers came to a similar conclusion when they
asked a group of study participants to complete an attention-
demanding task in which they had to find a number of hidden
characters on a screen as quickly as possible. Half had a cell phone
that was not theirs lying next to the screen, which they weren't
allowed to pick up. The other half had a small notepad lying on the
table. The results? Those with the notepad did best. The phone
seemed to steal the subjects' attention just by lying there.

Ignoring your phone is an active choice

On a subconscious level, the brain seems to be aware of the digital
draw of the phone in your pocket and has to spend a certain amount
of mental bandwidth ignoring it. As a result, your concentration isn't
what it could be. If you think about it, it's not very surprising. Dopamine tells your brain what's important and what you should focus
on. Your phone triggering a release of dopamine hundreds of times
a day will no doubt make you more interested in it.

Ignoring something is an active choice that requires the brain to
make an effort. You have probably noticed it yourself. When you are
sitting down for coffee with a friend, you put your phone on the
table—perhaps screen down to avoid distraction. Once you are

sitting there, in order to resist the impulse to pick it up, you have to keep thinking: *I'm not going to pick up my phone.* It's not surprising that your brain has to expend mental capacity ignoring something that serves up hundreds of little dopamine hits a day. After all, it has evolved to seek out anything that provides more dopamine.

When the brain has to put effort into resisting the pull of your phone, its capacity to perform other tasks decreases. It probably won't matter much if what you are doing doesn't require a lot of focus. But if you really need to concentrate, it can be a problem. Like when American researchers had their test subjects take a demanding concentration test, during which some of them received a text message or phone call from the test leaders that they weren't supposed to answer. It turned out that they still made more mistakes on the test—three times as many, in fact!

The same effect was observed when a number of study participants were asked to read a text in a Word document with plain formatting followed by another text where some of the words had been turned into hyperlinks. Afterward, when they had to answer questions about the texts they had just read, it turned out they had learned less from the text with links, even though they didn't click on them. The explanation is probably that the brain constantly has to make a decision—*should I click on the link or not?*—and each small decision takes up mental bandwidth, sapping both our limited power of concentration and our working memory. Just as the brain has to expend energy in order not to pick up the phone on the table, it takes energy not to click on the link.

Losing interest in your surroundings

Every time I'm having coffee or a meal with someone and they pick up their phone, I get annoyed—but I'm no better! There is a selfish reason why you should try to avoid doing this, besides the fact that other people are likely to appreciate it. There is a risk that you will find the conversation itself more boring if you keep your phone in front of you. Turns out, our phones are so seductive that they seem to make us less interested in others.

In one study, 30 people were asked to meet a stranger for ten minutes and talk about anything they wanted. They each sat on a chair with a table between them. Some were allowed to keep their phones on the table, others weren't. Afterward, they were asked to describe how interesting they thought the conversation had been. Those who'd had their phones in sight found the conversation less interesting and even thought their interlocutors were less trustworthy and empathetic. And to be clear, their phones were just lying there—they didn't even pick them up!

This isn't particularly surprising either. After all, dopamine tells us where to focus our attention! If there is an object in front of us that serves up thousands of little dopamine hits every day, naturally the brain will be drawn there. When we must resist the impulse to pick up our phones, our limited concentration is disrupted—as we know, ignoring it is an active choice—with the consequence that we don't follow the conversation.

The same phenomenon was observed by researchers examining how 300 people perceived a dinner with friends. Half of them had been told they would receive a text message during dinner and should therefore have their phones at hand. The others were asked not to have their phones out. Afterward, it turned out that those who had kept their phones close found the dinner less rewarding. The differences weren't vast, but they were clear. Simply put, if you keep your phone on the table in front of you, you will find others just a bit less interesting.

But surely having your phone out while waiting for a text message shouldn't ruin a whole dinner? Perhaps not, though the people in the study didn't exactly leave their phone on standby. Rather, they fiddled with it for more than 10 percent of the total dinner time—even though they only needed to keep it in front of them to reply to a text message.

The role of dopamine is to tell us what's important and what we should focus on, where "important" isn't getting good grades, climbing the career ladder or even feeling well, but strictly what made our ancestors survive and pass on their genes. Something as ingeniously designed as a cell phone can provide a tiny dopamine hit 300 times a day, and every time it tells you: *Focus on me!*

Is it so strange, then, that it's hard to stop thinking about your phone while at school or at work? Is it strange that you must expend precious mental bandwidth not to pick it up? Is it strange that your phone is so alluring that you lose interest in your dinner company? Is it strange that you feel stressed—even panicked—when you lose the thing that offers up new experiences and rewards every ten minutes? Not really, is it?

the mind-body method

How Moving Your Body Can Strengthen Your Mind

Dr. Anders Hansen

Zeitgeist • New York

CHAPTER 1

YOUR CHANGEABLE BRAIN

The chief function of the body is to carry the brain around.

THOMAS A. EDISON

IMAGINE YOU'RE sitting in a time machine and you've cranked the year back to 10,000 B.C. The machine starts clanging and suddenly you're hurled thousands of years back in time. You nervously step out of the capsule and look around. A group of people dressed in animal hides are standing there and they seem surprised to see you.

What is your first impression of them? That they're primitive cave dwellers who might, at best, be able to hunt down an animal and kill it, but who are otherwise incapable of showing any hint of advanced thought? One is tempted to think that, but as it happens you and they are very much alike. Of course, they don't speak the same language as you and they have a completely different set of experiences, but overall they function quite similarly to you. They possess the same cognitive abilities and the same feelings you do. We humans have not changed all that much, really, over the past 12,000 years.

By contrast, our lifestyle has undergone immense transformation in just 100 years, and if you look back as far as 12,000 years, the degree of change is unbelievable. You live in material comfort and make use of technical tools the likes of which your ancient predecessors could not have conceived in their wildest dreams. You exist in entirely different social environments. You probably meet as many fresh faces in a single week as they would over the course of their entire lives.

There is another fundamental difference between your way of life and that of those who came before you: they moved considerably more than you do. Taken in historical context, they are not alone in this. Over hundreds of thousands of years our ancestors were significantly more physically active than we are today, and the reason is simple: throughout most of human history it was necessary to be physically active in order to procure food and survive. Consequently, not only are our bodies built for movement, so are our brains.

Twelve thousand years seems like an eternity but from a biological perspective, it is a short period. Evolution often requires considerably more time than that for big changes to occur in a species, and this applies to us humans and our brain, too. Despite the enormous changes we have made to our lifestyle that have removed us farther and farther from the life we evolved for, our brain is still adapted to a life on the savanna. This is especially true when it comes to how much we move. Even though we don't need to hunt for our food anymore and can now order our groceries online, our brains still run more efficiently when we live a little more like our ancestors did—and when we move our bodies.

EXERCISE AND TRAINING PRODUCE A MORE EFFICIENT BRAIN

I've read thousands of studies over the years, and if I had to pick the one that fascinated me the most, the one that changed not only my view of medicine and health but also to a certain degree my view of life in general, it would be the one in which the brains of about one hundred 60-year-old human test subjects were examined by magnetic resonance imaging (MRI).

MRI is nothing short of a technical miracle for brain researchers; it is a tool that has truly opened us up to another world. Today, thanks to MRI, we can look inside the cranium and get a picture, in real time, of how the brain works while we think and perform different tasks, at no risk of injury to the person being examined.

The goal of this one particular study was to understand the effects of aging on the brain, because our brain—just like our skin, heart and lungs—does get old. But *how* does it age, really? And are we doomed to go through the aging process with no means of influencing it, or are we able to alter its course in any way, perhaps by engaging in regular physical activity? This is what researchers began to suspect after animal trials demonstrated that the brains of caged mice who could run on a wheel tended to age more slowly.

For the study's authors to answer these questions, the 60-year-old participants were split into two groups: one in which the subjects took regular walks a few times a week over the course of one year, and one in which the people met as often as the other group but performed easy exercises that did not increase their heart rate.

The test subjects' brains were examined by MRI prior to the study, and again one year after the study. To observe the participants' brain processes, the MRIs took place while the subjects were performing a set of psychological tests. The scans revealed how different parts of the brain were being activated, and how areas in the temporal lobe worked together with areas in the occipital lobe and the frontal lobe in what appeared to be a sophisticated network.

However, the most telling revelation lay not in the results per se, but in the contrast those results showed between the study's two test groups.

The participants who walked didn't just get in better shape over the course of the year, they also developed more effective brains. The MRIs showed that the connections between the lobes had strengthened, most notably the connections between the temporal lobe and both the frontal and occipital lobes. In short, different sections of the brain were better integrated with one another, which meant, quite simply, that the entire organ functioned more efficiently. Somehow the physical activity—i.e., the walks—had had a positive impact on the brain's connectivity pattern.

When the results from the 60-year-olds' MRI scans were compared to the younger participants' scans, the researchers found they looked similar. The brains of the 60-year-olds who had been physically active appeared to have become biologically younger. The most striking effect was the connection between the frontal and the temporal lobes, which is the area of the brain that tends to be most affected by aging. Seeing improvement in that particular area indicated that the aging process of the whole brain had stalled.

But more importantly, in addition to yielding measurable results on the scans the regular walks made a real, practical difference. Psychological tests showed that the set of cognitive functions called "executive control" or "executive function"—which among other things include the ability to take initiative, to plan and to have attentional control—showed improvement in the group of test subjects who regularly walked.

Simply put, this discovery indicates that the brain works more efficiently in people who are physically active, and that the effects of aging can be halted or even reversed to make the brain more energetic.

Take a minute to think about what you've just read. Go over it again. If that isn't enough to motivate you to start exercising, I don't know what will. You know that you'll improve your stamina by running and that you'll develop bigger muscles by lifting weights, but you probably weren't aware that exercise and training can also bring about changes in your brain—changes that are not only measurable by modern medical technology but are also extremely important to optimal cognitive function.

We're going to examine these changes in more detail later in this book, but first we're going to look at how the brain works, and then we'll see how it can be made to operate better.

YOUR INNER UNIVERSE

The brain has shown itself to be rather more malleable than we were led to believe until recently. What you have inside your cranium isn't some kind of advanced computer with genetically preprogrammed functions destined to develop in a certain way; the brain is far more complex than that. It contains approximately 86 billion (86,000,000,000) brain cells. Each cell can connect to thousands of other cells, which means that the number of possible connections in the brain totals at least 86 *trillion* (86,000 billion). That is about 500 times more than the number of stars in the Milky Way. To say that you have your own universe inside your skull might sound somewhat New Age-y, but it is actually an accurate metaphor.

Every sensation you experience, every thought you have—everything leaves a trace and changes you a little.

The universe in your head is enormously active. Old brain cells die and new cells are created continuously. Connections are made between the cells and connections are lost if they are not used. The strength of those connections changes over time depending on how the brain redesigns its architecture. You can look at the brain as a highly sophisticated ecosystem in a state of constant flux. These changes keep happening throughout your life, not only when you are a child or when you learn something new. Every sensation you experience, every thought you have—everything leaves a trace and changes you a little. The brain you have today is not quite the same as the one you had yesterday. The brain is a continuous *work in progress.*

It is *not*—as some believe—the number of brain cells or the size of the brain that determines whether a brain functions well. The most telling example is Albert Einstein, whose brain was neither bigger nor heavier than the average human brain. Einstein's brain weighed 2.7 pounds, compared to the average man's brain of 3 pounds and the average woman's brain, which weighs approximately 3.5 ounces less.

For a long time, I believed it was the number of connections between brain cells that determined the brain's capacity, but that's not right either. Two-year-old children have significantly more connections between brain cells than adults do. As a child grows, the number of connections decreases. This process is called "pruning," and it's estimated that up to 20 billion connections disappear *every 24 hours* from the age of two to adolescence. The brain weeds out unused connections to make room for the ones that carry signals—which can be neatly summarized as: *neurons that fire together, wire together.*

But if neither the number of brain cells nor the number of connections between them determines the quality of a brain, what does? The answer is that when we do different things—swimming, cycling or signing your name, for instance—the brain uses a type of "program" called a functional network. You have a program for swimming, another for cycling and a third for writing your signature. Everything you do is dependent on these networks, which are all basically built from a collection of brain cells that are connected to one another. A program can integrate cells from many different areas of the brain, and for it to run optimally—to enable you to swim, ride a bike or sign something—it is necessary for the brain's different areas to be closely interconnected.

Practice makes perfect—and more agile—brain programs

Imagine you'd like to learn to play a simple tune on the piano. Many different areas in the brain must work together to make that possible. You may start looking at the keys. A signal goes from the eyes through the optic nerve to the primary visual cortex in the occipital lobe. Simultaneously, the motor cortex (in the brain) must coordinate the movements of your hands and fingers. The auditory cortex processes sound information and sends it to areas called "association areas" in the temporal and parietal lobes. The information eventually reaches the frontal lobe, the seat of higher brain functions, and you become aware of what you are playing and can correct any wrong notes you hit. All this activity to play a simple piano tune!

All these areas in the visual and auditory centrums, the motor cortex, the parietal and frontal lobes are part of the brain's program for playing music. The more you practice, the better you become at it, and the more efficiently the program runs in your brain. At the beginning it will take a great deal of effort to play the tune. The program is inefficient and awkward and requires that big chunks of the brain be fully engaged in the task. That's why you'll experience playing the piano as mentally taxing and you will need to focus hard to accomplish the task.

In time, as you continue to practice, it will become easier; once you've put in a tremendous amount of work, you will be able to play the tune while thinking about something else. The brain's program for playing the tune has now become efficient at transferring information; a repeated signal through the network has strengthened the connection: *neurons that fire together, wire together.* In the end, less and less mental effort will be required, and you'll be able to play the tune without giving it a second thought.

As the program for playing the tune activates cells from different areas of the brain, those different areas need to be closely connected for the program to run well. We can compare it to a computer, where all the different components need to be connected in order to work. If the connections are bad, the computer won't run, even if each input works well independently.

The connections reveal how you live your life

It may sound a bit strange that different areas of the brain can be connected to each other to different degrees, but research has shown that this could be an important reason why cognitive abilities vary between people. Fascinating findings have recently been uncovered in this specific area of research.

Advanced brain testing on hundreds of individuals has revealed that different parts of the brain are closely interconnected in people with sets of qualities that are deemed to be "positive," such as good memory function and concentration, higher education and a cautious, negligible intake of alcohol and tobacco. In subjects with "negative" qualities, such as poor anger management, smoking and alcohol or drug abuse, the opposite pattern has been observed: these areas of the brain are badly connected to each other.

You can see roughly how a person leads their life by looking at their brain's connectivity pattern.

That many positive qualities leave an identical imprint on the brain, and that negative qualities seem to make the opposite type of mark, implies that there is a "positive–negative axis" along which we can all be placed depending on how we live. The scientists who performed this study believe that you can see roughly how a person leads their life by looking at their brain's connectivity pattern.

So is there anything else that's considered positive along that positive–negative axis, apart from good memory, higher education and caution around alcohol? Indeed there is: being in good physical shape.

YOUR LIFESTYLE SHAPES YOUR BRAIN

The debate about whether we are shaped by our genes or our environment has ebbed and flowed over a long time, often veering from one extreme point of view to another, more stringent opinion. Today we know it is *neither* our genetic makeup *nor* our environment that decides our fate exclusively, but a combination of both. We also know that genes and environment are closely interwoven: the environment affects our genes—our DNA—through incredibly complex biological mechanisms.

There are a few numbers that clearly illustrate that it isn't only your genetic makeup that decides how your brain will develop and how you will turn out as a human being. You possess approximately 23,000 genes. You also have about 86 billion brain cells, which in turn have around 86 trillion connections between them. Your 23,000 genes can't possibly hold sway over those 86 trillion connections. Quite simply, the brain is far too complex to be governed by an exact, predetermined

---

genetic program that is in charge of the brain's development throughout life.

Your genes set the stage for how your brain cells will be created and die, and how they will connect and disconnect from one another. Exactly how this happens, which characteristics you develop and how you function mentally will be influenced by your life experiences, by the type of environment you live in and, not least, by the lifestyle you adopt.

The aspect of our lifestyle that this book is all about—physical exercise—is, naturally, not the only factor that influences how our brain develops, but research shows that it plays a pivotal role and is far more important than most are aware of.

Judgmental research?

You might believe that this type of research is judgmental or elitist; after all, the mere fact that we are talking about a positive–negative axis suggests a sort of ranking of people. I completely understand how it could be interpreted that way, but I also believe that some people may misconstrue the results of these tests. Our *inherent qualities* are not what primarily affect our brain's connectivity pattern, nor where we happen to be situated along the positive–negative axis. Instead, it is our lifestyle that does this. Through the *choices* we make, we can change our brain's operating mode on a more fundamental level than we previously thought. It isn't just our brain that decides how we think and act; our thoughts and actions can also modify our brain and how it works. We run our brains, not the other way around. From this angle, we can see how the most important thing for improving the connection between different parts of our brain might be to partake in regular physical exercise, and how being in good physical condition produces a positive reading on the positive–negative axis.

NEUROPLASTICITY: HOW THE BRAIN CHANGES THROUGHOUT LIFE

I wish I had learned to play an instrument as a kid. Now it's too late.
Many of us have had this thought at one time or another. The fact is, the brain is extremely malleable during childhood, which makes learning everything from languages to motor skills swift and natural. But why is it that a child's brain can learn so much in such a short time, with little obvious effort?

A youngster must quickly learn to navigate the world. This is evident in their brain from the cells' enormous ability not only to create connections with one another but also to break them off (i.e., pruning). This happens at a rate that will, as you've noticed, never come back later in life. The brain's capacity for change—which in scientific parlance is referred to as "neuroplasticity"—is perhaps its most important quality, because even if its flexibility is never as great as when we are children, it doesn't vanish entirely. It's still there— even in adults, even in 80-year-olds. To see exactly how influenceable and changeable an adult brain is, we're going to look at what happened to Michelle Mack, a 42-year-old American woman whose remarkable life story has changed our understanding of what the human brain is truly capable of.

The woman who only had half her brain

Michelle Mack was born in Virginia in November 1973. As early as a few weeks after her birth, her parents noticed something was not right. Michelle was unable to steady her gaze and she didn't move normally, especially her right arm and leg. Her parents took her to numerous specialists to examine her eyes and to see if she had cerebral palsy, which she did not. None of the neurologists they consulted could explain Michelle's symptoms, and neither could an X-ray of her brain. In the early 1970s, our modern technologies—such as the computerized axial tomography (CAT) scan and MRI—were still in the early stages of development.

At the age of three, Michelle still wasn't walking and she could hardly speak. Her physician recommended that they schedule a new CAT scan, since medical diagnostic techniques had advanced since her first examination.

The result of the scan performed in 1977 shocked Michelle's parents and her physicians. Michelle was missing virtually the entire left side of her brain, probably due to something that had happened to her while she was still an embryo. She was living with only half a brain.

One possible explanation is that Michelle had suffered a stroke before birth; another is that her left carotid artery had been blocked, depriving the left side of her brain of blood. No one could provide a definitive answer, but one thing was crystal clear: more than 90 percent of the left side of Michelle's brain was missing.

The left side of the brain is commonly thought of as the analytical and rational part, the seat of mathematical and linguistic thinking, while the right side is more artistic and creative. Even though we now realize that this divvying up of the brain is an oversimplification, it isn't too far from reality. Bearing in mind the set of responsibilities held by the left side of the brain, many of Michelle's difficulties suddenly made sense. Her inability to speak properly could be explained by the missing linguistic part of her brain. And since the left side of the brain would also have been in charge of the mobility of the right side of the body (and vice versa), it was no wonder she had trouble moving her right arm and leg.

However, it isn't Michelle's early years that make her so fascinating, but what happened to her later. She successively developed the abilities she had been lacking, and at a rate her physicians had not dared hope for. She learned to walk, speak and read, and she otherwise developed somewhat normally, if a little more slowly than most of her peers.

Today Michelle lives a normal life in many ways and works part time in her parish. Her ability to find words is mostly normal, even though that function is usually found in the part of the brain that she is missing. Although the mobility in her right arm and leg is still limited, she has no problem walking.

Tests have shown that Michelle has some difficulty with abstract thinking, but she has a phenomenal memory for detail. This gives her a highly unusual skill: she can immediately tell you what day of the week corresponds with a randomly selected date. Ask Michelle what day of the week March 18, 2010 fell on and she'll correctly answer "Thursday" almost instantly.

The right half of Michelle's brain has taken over handling many of the tasks her left brain would normally deal with. We know from past studies that this can be done on a smaller scale, but few scientists had speculated that such a massive restructuring of the brain—one that could compensate for a missing half—was possible. The rewiring of Michelle's brain is so extensive that her brain's right half actually looks a bit crowded. In fact, Michelle has issues with visuospatial orientation, i.e., the ability to judge distance and spatial orientation. Visuospatial orientation is normally found in the right side of the brain (which is intact for Michelle), but it is believed that since her right brain is pulling double duty—handling responsibilities for both the right and the missing left side—there just isn't enough room in there for all its regular functions.

It's probably no accident that Michelle can immediately match a specific date to its corresponding day of the week. The two halves of our brain work as a kind of brake for each other and, as strange as it may sound, inhibit the function of the other half. Why would the brain limit itself? It could be to restrain the other half if it grows too strong within a certain area, so that we achieve balance in our cerebral abilities and acquire reasonable abilities in many areas, instead of becoming extremely adept at some and very poor at others. But if the halves of the brain are unable to communicate, the equilibrium might be lost and then certain abilities can blossom, often to the detriment of others.

The human Google

This is exactly what is believed to have happened to the American Kim Peek, the inspiration for Dustin Hoffman's role as Raymond Babbitt in the movie *Rain Man*. Kim was born with an injury to the corpus callosum, a band of nerve fibers that forms the most important link between the left and right sides of the brain. Kim's injury caused a faulty connection in this link, and so he didn't learn to walk until he was four years old. He was considered to be so severely mentally disabled that doctors suggested he be institutionalized.

But just like Michelle, Kim recovered and developed in ways no one could have foreseen. At around five years old he learned to read, and whenever he finished a book he placed it front cover down. His parents were astonished at the speed with which the house filled up with down-facing books. By then Kim was also beginning to show a mind-boggling memory for detail, perhaps the best ever documented in a human being. He could read two pages of a book simultaneously, the left side with his left eye and the right side with his right eye. It took him ten seconds to read one page; he could go through an entire book in an hour. His favorite pastime was going to the public library, where he read eight books a day.

Kim remembered everything in the approximately 12,000 books he had read. He kept in his head an unimaginable number of facts of varying degrees of importance about everything from Shakespeare to American zip codes to the British royal family. If anyone deserves to be called the "human Google," it's Kim Peek.

As with Michelle Mack, Kim could also immediately tell you which weekday a date corresponded to, whether it was several decades in the future or in the past. People often told Kim their date of birth and asked him what day it was. Not only did he immediately give them the correct answer—"You were born on a Sunday" —but he could also add, "You will turn 80 on a Friday."

Kim's abilities were so unique that he has been called "Kimputer" and "mega-savant," but his life was far from simple. He was often awkward in social situations and was barely able to dress himself. He also tested quite a bit below average on IQ tests, despite his extraordinary memory. Kim was always generous and volunteered his time whenever neuroscientists asked him to, and his unique case has provided us with important clues about how memory works. It is now believed that Kim's outsized memory was a result of his brain's halves lacking the ability to balance each other out.

THE BRAIN'S PROGRAMS CAN BE REWRITTEN

There are similarities as well as differences between Kim Peek and Michelle Mack. In Michelle's case the connection between the two halves of her brain was not absent—half her brain was simply not there. But the missing half might very well have had the same effect as a bad link between two existing brain halves, ensuring that certain abilities grew uncontrollably and gave rise to exceptional qualities.

Michelle and Kim are perhaps the best examples of neuroplasticity— the brain's superb ability to reorganize itself—and there's no longer any doubt that the brain's structure and operating mode are changeable, not only for Michelle and Kim, but also for you and me.

But why have I devoted so much time to these two people's stories in a book about the effects of exercise and athletic training on the brain? The reason is very simple: it is important to show that the brain *can* change, because not everyone is aware of this. So what creates this change? This is how we end up on the topic of exercise.

There are few things as effective in making the brain changeable as being physically active.

DO WE ONLY USE 10 PERCENT OF OUR BRAIN?

It's time to put to rest the myth that we only use 10 percent of our brain. It's not unreasonable to think that you might only be using 10 percent of your brain while reading this sentence. It's also not impossible that you might only use 10 percent of your brain when you go for a bike ride, although it's not necessarily the same 10 percent you press into service when you're reading. In actuality, we work our entire brain—but different parts of it depending on what we're up to.

Today we know that electrical activity and the use of glucose and oxygen—the brain's main fuels—are continuous processes in the brain. This means it is always active; no area is idle in a healthy brain. The brain would never allow 90 percent of its capacity to stay dormant. Considering our brain's phenomenal ability to move different functions around (just think back to Michelle Mack), it would quickly put any quiet area to good use.

The idea that we only use 10 percent of our brain is also obviously a myth when we account for energy consumption. The brain devours a substantial amount of energy—about 20 percent of all the energy required by the body—even though it only makes up 2 percent of our body's total weight. This means that it uses more than ten times the energy per pound than the rest of the body. From an evolutionary standpoint, such an energy-draining organ wouldn't have been permitted to grow if it were unnecessary. The cost of a large brain is that it requires more food, and thus more time is needed to seek out this food. If the brain were indeed 90 percent inactive, the time and energy expended to find food would be a huge misuse of resources. Such a wastrel would not have survived long on the path of natural selection.

MORE LIKE MODELING CLAY THAN CHINA

In the study of neuroplasticity, it has been shown that there are few things as effective in making the brain changeable—that is, neuroplastic—as being physically active. It also appears that the activity does not need to last an especially long time. The fact is, just 20–30 minutes is enough to affect neuroplasticity.

One of the mechanisms that converts your running steps into a changeable brain involves an amino acid called gamma-aminobutyric acid (GABA). GABA acts like a brake on the brain, inhibiting activity and making sure nothing changes. But GABA's influence ebbs when you become physically active, because exercise removes its block against change, thus making the brain more flexible and better at reorganizing itself. If we consider the brain from a "more like modeling clay than china" perspective, the change in GABA activity makes the clay softer and more malleable. Thus the brain of a person who exercises becomes more like a child's, and GABA is involved in that process.

Hopefully you have realized by now how changeable the brain is, and that exercise plays a big role in this changeability since it can modify and streamline our brain's programs. Results become apparent in many different areas, and we will now look a bit more closely at those areas, specifically at the impact that exercise has on our mental functions. We'll start with something that afflicts many people today: stress and anxiety.

ABOUT THE AUTHOR

Dr. Anders Hansen is a Swedish psychiatrist, speaker and international bestselling author with his own TV series exploring the human brain. Dr. Hansen's books have sold millions of copies globally and topped bestseller lists around the world. He is the winner of the book of the year Big Health Award 2017 and 2019, and Sweden's Mensa Prize 2018.

Dr. Hansen is also the author of *The ADHD Advantage*, *The Attention Fix* and *The Mind-Body Method*.

Hi there,

We hope *The Happiness Cure* helped you.
If you have any questions or concerns about your book,
or have received a damaged copy, please contact
customerservice@penguinrandomhouse.com.
We're here and happy to help.

Also, please consider writing a review on your favorite retailer's
website to let others know what you thought of the book.

Sincerely,
The Zeitgeist Team